GOD'S
Possibility
to MAN'S
Impossibility

SILVESTRE GUERRIDO, M.ED.

Copyright © 2014 by Silvestre Guerrido, M.Ed.

God's Possibility to Man's Impossibility
by Silvestre Guerrido, M.Ed.

Printed in the United States of America

ISBN 9781629526980

All rights reserved solely by the author. The author guarantees all contents are original and do not infringe upon the legal rights of any other person or work. No part of this book may be reproduced in any form without the permission of the author. The views expressed in this book are not necessarily those of the publisher.

Unless otherwise indicated, Bible quotations are taken from the New King James Version (NKJV). Copyright © 1982 by Thomas Nelson, Inc. Used by permission. All rights reserved.

www.xulonpress.com

FOREWORD

If you believe that miracles are for Christians, or for people with faith only, you are sadly mistaken. If that would be the case, there would be no Christians in the world. Each one of us was once lost. We all have sinned, and come short of the glory of God (Ro. 3:23), and born in sin (Psalm 51:5). It was by the great miracle of salvation, through faith and grace from Jesus Christ, that we were saved (Eph. 2:8-10).

For decades, we preachers have emphasized the need for faith for people to receive miracles. No faith, no miracles. Well, do you know that out of thirty-plus miracles in the NT, only ten required faith from those receiving the miracles?

> *John 5:1-9 (the lame man healed at the pool of Bethesda); Matt. 8:2-4 (a leper healed); Matt. 9:2-8 (a man sick of the palsy is healed); John 9:1-7 (a blind man healed); Matt. 20:29-34 (two blind men healed); Matt. 9:20-22, Mk. 5:24-34 (the woman with the issue of blood); Matt. 14:24-33 (Peter walks on water); Lu. 5:1-11, John 21:1-11 (the catching of many fish), and Lu. 17:11-14 (ten lepers are healed).*

The other twenty miracles happened to people who had no faith, or were not Christians; people who received miracles because of the faith of others, people hand-picked by Jesus, and friends who received miracles because they were in the right place at the right time. I'll illustrate some examples of these miracles in the Bible, and then, I challenge you to continue enriching yourself with the loving grace of Jesus Christ and the love of God:

Mk. 2:4-5, Matt. 8:5-13 (a man is healed because of the faith of others); Luke 6:17-19 (Jesus healed the multitude [ALL] out of compassion; Lu. 9:11 (Jesus healed a multitude in need of healing); Matt. 15:30 (Jesus healed sick brought in by friends); John 18:10, Matt. 26:51-53 (Jesus healed an enemy of Christians); Lu. 8:26-39 (Jesus healed a demon-possessed man without the man asking; the demon spoke to Jesus, not the man); John 5:1-15 (Jesus hand-picked a man to be healed).

In dealing with miracles, one must not forget what Jesus' ministry is all about: to preach the gospel to the poor, to heal the brokenhearted, to preach deliverance to the captive, and recovering of sight to the blind, and to set at liberty them that are bruised (Lu. 4:18).

Jesus was not talking about the "saved," or the "Christian," but about the destitute, the afflicted, the humble, the spirit-crumpled, the bruised and the oppressed. Weren't we all in that predicament at one time in our lives? But we are not going to limit ourselves to the miracles that happened in the Bible. Miracles are for today also, because Jesus is alive.

Foreword

One of the greatest misconceptions of the Bible is to say that God doesn't hear the sinner (John 9:31); not true. If we accept that as a true premise, then the Bible is contradicting itself. One very important fact about the Bible is that all its statements are statements of truth, but are not truly stated. Let me explain.

They are statements of truth because someone spoke them, and the people spoke what they truly believed, based on their own experience. But they are not truly stated simply because many times these statements were attributed to Christ, when in reality the statements might not have been the way that Jesus thought or spoke.

If we say that God doesn't hear the sinner, then we can also say that God doesn't heal the sinner, or that miracles are not for sinners, which we have already established as not being true. We will be negating, nullifying the purpose, the mission of the Gospel (Lu. 4:18).

Jesus Himself commanded us to love our enemies, to bless them that curse us, to do good to them that hate us, and to pray for them which despitefully use us, and persecute us, that we may be the children of our Father which is in heaven (and listen what he says next): for He makes His sun to rise on the evil and the good, and sends rain on the just and the unjust (Matt.5:44-45). Jesus will never ask us to do anything He himself would not do.

Rain can be a miracle in a drought season. And when it rains, it rains on the just, as well as on the unjust. God makes no difference. If He doesn't, why do we?

The Bible says that faith comes by hearing, and hearing by the word of God (Ro. 10:17). That's the great miracle of salvation. We are saved because we heard when He spoke to us, and He heard us when we answered, while we were yet sinners. We all have sinned, and come short of the glory of God (Ro. 3:23). And it was in our state of sin that God heard us, and saved us.

At times, we all need to see to believe. We all have a little of Thomas in us; we doubt. If God needs a miracle to make anyone believe that He is, that's what He will do. He did it with us, right? When we were yet sinners. One of the most beautiful parables in the Bible is the parable of the lost sheep:

The man had one hundred sheep, but lost one. He left the other ninety-nine in the wilderness, risking losing them, to find the lost sheep. And when he found it, he made merry; he had a feast. That's what Christ does for the sinner; that's what He did for each one of us, when we were still sinners. That's the miracle of salvation for sinners. Miracles are for sinners, too (Luke 15:4-7).

Miracles: God's Possibility to Man's Impossibility will account present day miracles, miracles that happened, and are happening to common people, just like you and me. People with faith, people with little faith, good people in need of God, and in need of a miracle. It could be you. Wouldn't you like to be part of a miracle today? Jesus can do it, and you can receive it. There's a miracle waiting for you!!

INTRODUCTION

I was born and raised in Puerto Rico. I came to the USA at the age of twenty-five. I joined and served in the US Army for twenty-two years, and was able to complete a master's degree in education from National-Louis University with a 4.0 GPA. By reading this book, you are becoming a witness to a miracle. When you read this book, just "feel" what the Spirit [of God] is saying.

****

If you are like me, you would open the table of contents of a book, find the peak of the story and go right to it, missing… the rest of the story!

Impatience could make you miss important details that could lead to the peak of the story. If you get to the peak before knowing how you got there, the peak will no longer be the high point, but just an end without a means.

Imagine getting married without the excitement of a courtship! What stories would you have to tell your children? How would you come to know your partner if you never got in touch with his/her inner person; the real person? And I am not talking about living together outside of marriage. When I say partner, I am talking about a man and a woman living in marriage. You may be joining a stranger instead of a friend, and it will be too late to find out once you are married.

Most of the fun and intrigue in a story is found in the chapters that precede the peak. It's of most importance to find the way to get there, for you to get there. You may never get to a point if you don't know how to get to that point; you'll find yourself lost, like I got lost sometimes in the Autobahn in Germany. Believe me, it was no fun to find the way out, especially if you couldn't read the German signs!

As a test to your patience (or impatience), I decided to place the table of contents in the middle of the book. Let's see if you can contain yourself from going to the table of contents and finding the *Greatest Miracle of All* chapter before you read the book!

THE PURPOSE OF MIRACLES

The real purpose of miracles is to glorify God; to establish the love, the power and the presence of God in our lives, and to give testimony of the person of Jesus Christ as the Messiah, the Sent One, the Savior, and the Way to the Father.

When I talk about miracles, I'm referring to those supernatural occurrences that boggle the minds of people, both believers and non-believers. I'm talking about those events that challenge and defy the stability of the universe; those acts of God that transcend human intelligence and science and counteract natural laws and cause people, believers and non-believers, to believe that truly there is a greater being, alone capable of performing these acts.

Miracles do not violate natural laws, but rather counteract the laws. It is simply a greater law superseding another law. Gravity says that what goes up, must come down. Yet, there is a greater law. The law of aerodynamics says that given the right size, shape and speed, gravity can be counteracted.

Every time that a shuttle goes into space; every time that an airplane takes off into the air, and remains there, is the result of a greater law counteracting another law. The law of gravity had been counteracted by a greater law, the law of aerodynamics. No law has been violated; rather, it has been counteracted by a greater law. *(httpp://www.christiananswers.net/dictionary/miracle.html.)*

It's simply a greater force, the divine force of God counteracting another force, the law of man, or the law of nature. Where man says it cannot happen, God says yes, it can.

It's proof that the divine law or force of God has preeminence and superseding power over any physical law of the universe. And, let's not forget that it was God who established the natural laws in the universe for our benefit, so miracles are no more than God effecting greater laws over His first natural laws.

Many give this being different names. But His name is God, Jehovah, the Everlasting Father, the Ancient of Days, the King of Kings, the Lord of Lords, the Prince of Peace, the Almighty God; the Healer, the Provider, The Messiah, Jesus Christ. And each one of these names reveals His nature.

The Bible documents the occurrence of many of these supernatural acts of God. It's the divine intervention of God, both in the Old and New Testaments. These miracles in the Bible were not intended for people to believe in the prophets associated with the miracles, but in the God of the prophets, The Lord Jesus Christ.

Rather, they are undeniable proof of the existence and supremacy of God in the Old Testament, and of the divine mission of Jesus Christ as the incarnated Son of God; the Savior and Redeemer of the world in the New Testament, and that indeed the God of the Bible, the God of the impossible was with the prophets, working through them, making the impossible, possible.

The miracles of Moses in Egypt had the purpose of teaching Pharaoh God was the God over all, and not Pharaoh. Peter walking on water was to show that Jesus was the Christ, the Anointed One, and that He had power over the elements.

The miracle of Hannah giving birth to the Prophet Samuel (1 Sam. 1:1-28) happened for the glory of God, to show that God had the power to open and close wombs.

Hannah was one of Elkanah's wives. Elkanah was from the tribe of Ephraim, and as the custom was, he came yearly with his family from Ramathaim-zophim, his city, to offer sacrifices to the Lord in the temple in Shiloh. Eli was the High Priest at Shiloh. Hannah was barren; she could not have children. The Bible says that God had closed her womb. Peninnah, Elkanah's other wife, made constant provocation of Hannah; she made her feel miserable. But Elkanah loved Hannah more than Peninnah, because she was very humble.

One evening after supper, Hannah went to the temple, to pray to God for a child. When Hannah asked the Lord for a child, she also made a vow to the Lord, offering this child to Him, if He gave her a male child (v. 11). The Lord heard Hannah, and she conceived.

Samuel was born to Hannah; she kept her promise to God. When the child was weaned, Hannah took him to the tabernacle and left him with Eli the priest. Samuel became the greatest prophet of God and the last judge over Israel. Samuel was born to Hannah, not for her, but for the Lord. Again, a miracle happened for the glory of God.

The prophets of the New Testament emphasized the miraculous of God in their lives, rather than the miracles. Miracles in the New Testament are a plea from God to us as a definite, beyond question, proof of Jesus' divinity:

"For the Father loves the Son, and shows Him all things that He Himself does; and He will show Him greater works than these, that you may marvel" (John 5:20, NKJ).

The possibility and truth of miracles are established by the witness and testimony of those who experienced the miracles. However unbelievers, atheists will always deny the possibility of miracles, simply because they do not believe in the divine power of God.

(http://christiananswers.net/dictionary/miracle.html.)

Now, this is a funny thing: They believe facts of history and science based on the testimony of credible scientists and historians, but they do not believe in miracles based on the credible testimony of those who experienced these miracles!

Should we get angry or disappointed if miracles that we pray and believe for do not happen? No! We must remember that the purpose of miracles is not to please us, but to establish the divinity of Jesus Christ, and the will and supremacy of God, and that They are One (John 10:30, 38; 14:10).

The Apostle Paul, who by divine inspiration wrote almost two-thirds of the New Testament, prayed for God to remove from him a "thorn" in his flesh. No one can really say what this thorn, this intense affliction was, but we know that it had been put on him by a satanic entity, and that it was causing colossal spiritual, and perhaps physical, pain in Paul (2 Corinthians, 12:7-9).

It was so intense that Paul asked not once, but three times of the Lord that this affliction might depart from him. But the Lord answer to Paul was, "My grace is sufficient for you, for my strength is made perfect in weakness" (vs. 9).

Was Paul angry because God did not give him what he wanted? Absolutely not! Rather, it affirmed in him the power of God's grace, the persuasion that no matter how great the trial or the affliction, the grace of God would always be sufficient for him to do what God called him to do, and be victorious, even in the midst of trials and pain. And the grace of God will always be sufficient for us, too.

Jesus never promised of a tribulation-free world; on the contrary, He let us know that tribulation would come, but He also gave us the way out of tribulation: Himself!

"These things I have spoken to you, that in me you may have peace. In the world you will have tribulation; but be of good cheer [trust me]: I have overcome the world" (John 16:33, NKJ).

The disciples had the purpose to show that Jesus had power over death. His miracles of raising Lazarus and others from the dead showed that indeed we all will be raised from the dead in the last day. These miracles were only a premonition, an affirmation of the future resurrection of the people of God.

Death is one of the most difficult obstacles for Christians to overcome; God knows that. Jesus calls death the last enemy. It would have been very difficult for some of us to believe we can be raised from the dead, if we had not seen it. Although all of them died again physically, Jesus established His purpose: we all will be raised from the dead!

When the man was healed by the power of God in Peter and John, at the gate called Beautiful, he held on to them. When the people saw the man hanging on to them, they ran together to Peter and John, marveling at what just had taken place. When Peter and John perceived what these men were doing, they immediately proceeded to give the glory to God for the miracle:

"Men of Israel, why do you marvel at this, or why look so intently at us, as though by our own power or godliness we have made this man to walk? The God of Abraham, Isaac and Jacob, the God of our fathers glorified His Servant Jesus, whom you delivered up and denied in the presence of Pilate, when he was determined to let Him go.

"But you denied the Holy One and the Just, and asked for a murderer to be granted to you, and killed the Prince of life, whom God raised from the dead, of which we are witnesses.

And His name, through faith in His name, has made this man strong, whom you see and know. Yes, the faith which comes through Him has given him this perfect soundness in the presence of you all" (Acts 3:12-16, NKJ).

It was the disciples' intention to glorify Jesus, and to give evidence of His power and presence and love in their lives through the miracles, and not to lead the people to believe in them (the disciples) because of the miracles.

People look for miracles because they want God to help them in times of trouble. I think that when in trouble, almost everyone believes in God, or at least calls on His name; even unbelievers. God has always promised to be with His people [protection] in times of trouble. Ps. 46:1 says:

"God is our refuge and strength, a very present help in trouble."

In the Book of Judges, we find Gideon calling out to God:

"Oh, my Lord, if the LORD is with us, why then has all this happened to us? And where are all His miracles which our fathers told us about, saying, 'Did not the LORD bring us up from Egypt? But now the Lord has forsaken us, and delivered us into the hands of the Midianites" (Jud. 6:13, NKJ).

When Gideon saw trouble coming, he remembered the Lord his God, the Holy One of Israel, the One who parted the Red Sea and delivered Israel from the hands of Pharaoh.

To the faithless mind, however, miracles are still not the work of the divine intervention of God, but rather astronomical, astrological, or coincidental events.

Some argue that the Red Sea did not part, but that because of atmospheric or astronomical influences, the sea was only a couple of inches deep; Israel was able to cross the sea, but Egypt drowned [in a couple inches deep!].

Well, that makes God and this miracle even bigger, because God was able to drown thousands in only a couple inches of water; what a God!

Many Christians believe that science contradicts and rejects the existence of God.

However, I believe that science does not reject the existence of God; rather, it cannot disprove it, simply because God cannot be tested in a lab. If science could put God in a test tube and test Him in a lab, science will believe in God as a product of science; but God is not a product of science. God is...God! But He can only be believed in by faith. The proof of God: Himself!

Man refuses to believe in the fundamental laws of the universe, or the laws of God. In a recent article in "news.yahoo.com," (7/11/2006) titled, "Scientists Question Nature's Fundamental Laws," it is said that, and I quote:

"Public confidence in the 'constants' of nature may be at an all-time low. Recent research has found that the value of certain fundamental parameters, such as the speed of light or the invisible glue that holds nuclei together, might have been different in the past.

"'There is absolutely no reason these constants should be constant,' says astronomer Michael Murphy of the University of Cambridge. Then, he says,

"'These are famous numbers in physics, but we have no real reason for why they are what they are.'"

Well, they have no real reason for why these constants are what they are, simply because they don't want to believe in the One who makes the constants be constant, in the One that holds all things together, including the nuclei: God!

God is the God of constancy, steadiness, consistency, and everything that has to do with order. He is the glue that holds nuclei together; more than that, He is the creator of the nuclei!

But thank God that even science has some sense; sometimes!

Theorist Carlos Martins, also of the University of Cambridge says, "It doesn't make sense to talk about change of speed of light or electron charge."

But it makes a lot of sense to talk about the One who controls the speed of light, and holds the nuclei and electrons and the entire universe together. Miracles have been with us from the beginning. Life, all life began with a miracle.

MIRACLES

Miracles: the wonderful, supernatural, divine works of God. Nothing can humble the spirit of man as miracles do. When miracles happen, it is God as the origin of such wonders; it is God working supernaturally in a natural world.

Josephus, the great Jewish historian, 37 A.D., called Jesus the *Miracle Maker*, 'a doer of wonderful works.' Nicodemus, a man from the Pharisees, and a member of the Sanhedrin, the religious ruling body of Jews in Israel in Jesus' time, also acknowledged Jesus' miracles. He came to Jesus at night and said to Him:

"Rabbi, we know that You are a teacher come from God; for no one can do these *signs* [miracles] that you do unless God is with him" (John 3:2, NKJ).

Everyone expects miracles. They may call miracles by other names: coincidence, wish, or good luck. But everybody expects miracles. Some bigger and some smaller; but everybody looks out for miracles.

Every expectation of something greater beyond our control is an expectation for a miracle. We don't know how it is going to happen, but we *know* that it's going to happen. That is expectancy for a miracle!

When we know the car payment is due and we don't have the money but somehow *know* the payment is going to be on time; that is expectancy for a miracle!

When we know we'll put our children through college even when we are just making ends meet and are up to our necks in debt; that is expectancy for a miracle! But not all miracles happen when you need them. And sometimes miracles, especially the ones you pray for, do not happen at all!

Miracles just happen; not at our wish, but at the will of God. We pray for His will and believe. The rest is in God's hands. Miracles are the ultimate work and will of God and will happen in God's time because His time is always perfect, and miracles will happen for His glory. He knows what we need even before we know (Jer. 1:5; 29:11-13).

I'm not saying we don't pray for miracles. The Bible commands us to always pray (Luke 18:1), to pray without ceasing (1 Thess. 5:17), to pray everywhere (1 Tim. 2:8), and to pray one for another (Jas. 5:16). Prayer is communication with God. Prayer is the key to unlock heaven for us.

When some Jews repented at Peter's sermon after the Holy Spirit fell upon him and those in the Upper Room, the Bible say they continued steadfastly in the apostles' doctrine and fellowship, and in breaking of bread, and in *prayers,* and that many *wonders* and *signs* were done by the apostles. In other words, miracles happened because of their unity and *prayers* (Acts 2:42-43).

We pray in adoration and worship to God and for a relationship with Him; we pray for His will to be done, because His will is perfect. We pray for His kingdom to be established on earth ahead of our own interests. We pray for our present needs; we pray for His forgiveness, and we pray for His deliverance out of the hands of the enemy.

That's how Jesus taught His disciples to pray when they asked Him to teach them to pray. He taught them to pray in this manner:

> Our Father in heaven,
> Hallowed be your name.
> Your kingdom come,
> Your will be done,
> On earth as it is in heaven.
> Give us day by day our daily bread
> And forgive us our sins,
> For we also forgive everyone who
> Is indebted to us,
> And do not lead us into temptation,
> But deliver us from the evil one" (Lu. 11:1-4, NKJ).

That's how Jesus wants us to pray. Jesus' intention is not for us to repeat this prayer word by word, as a ritual, but rather to use it as a guide on how to address the Father when we pray.

God knows what we need before we pray and He will give us what we need, not necessarily what we want. Truthfully, I believe that most of the time we are able to provide for ourselves what we want, but not what we need. If we were able to always provide what we need, we would not need Him!

Perhaps at the time of our prayer, what we need is not a miracle, but a relationship with God, with Jesus. You see, when we have a relationship with Him, we have everything. Tell God what you *need*, but ask Him for His will.

The miracles that did not happen

My mother and I were best friends. In 1962, when I was ten years old, my best friend got seriously ill. She would spend the next three years of her life moving from hospital to hospital, looking for her healing, and looking for her miracle. I earnestly prayed to God for *that* miracle, in the way I knew to pray at the age of ten. I wanted so much to see her well!

But *that* miracle never happened. At the young age of forty-six, she died. I was thirteen. I cried daily for many years after her death, not understanding how God *could do that to her... and to me*. My mother was a hard-working, God- and people-loving woman! She really was my father's helpmeet, helping him to raise my siblings and me, five of us, by cooking for construction workers and teachers in my home town. Everybody loved her...and her cooking!

When I prayed for my mother's healing, she was not healed; she died! I was very angry with God; I blamed Him for her death. But later on, when I became a man, I understood that God did perform a miracle, but not the one I prayed for. The miracle was not that she lived, but that she died.

God spared her from evil. It was not what I prayed for, but it was God's best for my mother. God knows what the best thing is for each one of us. He *saved* [spared] my mother from evil; His *will* was done. He loved her, and He saved her from more suffering. Isaiah 57:1 says,

"The righteous perish, and no man takes it to heart; Merciful men are taken away, while no one considers that the righteous is taken away from evil" (NKJ).

Because He loved her, God spared my mother from the evil of a prolonged illness. But as a child, I did not understand it.

David and Bathsheba

God called David the apple of His eye, the man after God's own heart. David was the great king of Israel. God loved David, but David sinned against God. He abused his power as king and took Bathsheba, the wife of another man, and committed adultery with her, while the woman's husband, Uriah, was at war fighting for his king, David. Bathsheba conceived and had a child by David. God's anger kindled against David. He struck the child, and the child became ill. David pleaded with God for the child's life. For seven consecutive days he fasted and prostrated himself all night long before the Lord in prayer, hoping for a miracle.

But the miracle did not happen. After seven days, the child died (2 Sam.12:14-19). David repented and was forgiven by God, but the consequence of his sin prevailed. David prayed in earnest to God; he believed in God. You will not always get what you want, but you will always get the righteousness for what you do. Again, pray to God for His will for your life.

Jesus in Gethsemane

Miracles are to glorify God, not to satisfy man. Miracles are one way for God to show that He is in control and not us. Miracles happen when man can't do it. When man is out of resources and recognizes that what he needs, only God can do it, miracles will happen. You will not get what you ask for always. If what you ask for will not glorify God, it may not happen. It's not about you, but it's about God. Let me show you what I mean.

Jesus was sent to earth by the Father for one purpose only: to glorify God by redeeming man from sin through His death and resurrection. It was a hard thing to do, a hard death; a death undeserved by the One without sin.

The Gospels of Matthew, Mark and Luke have the narrative of Jesus in Gethsemane. I like Mark's version best, simply because it brings a more realistic perspective of the burden Jesus must have felt as the *man* God. When Jesus was praying in the Garden of Gethsemane, He asked God to remove the task from Him,

"Abba, Father, all things are possible for You. Take this cup away from *Me*; *nevertheless*, not what I will, but what You will" (Mk. 14:36, NKJ).

It was like He was saying: "Father, You can save Y*our* people any way you want; You are God. It doesn't have to be Me. Find another way, or another man." But Jesus, the *Son* of God, did not receive what He asked for.

I can imagine that there was a lapse of time, a waiting period between the moment Jesus said *Me*, and the moment

He said *nevertheless* in Mark 14:36. But the answer Jesus was waiting for did not come. He didn't get what He asked for because His request came out of His flesh, and not from His spirit; but the will of God was done.

His request would not bring God the glory. And when Jesus recognized it, He humbled Himself and asked for the will of the Father, and not His desire, to be done. And right there, in Gethsemane, thanks to the *greatest miracle of all*, the greatest decision of all time took place, and our lives were saved from eternal damnation.

WHO MAY RECEIVE MIRACLES?

As I stated previously, I don't believe miracles are only for Christians. I believe that unbelievers can also receive miracles. I define unbelievers as people who have not confessed Jesus as Savior and Lord. People with no faith, or with little faith; people who are in the right place at the right time, and even people chosen by Christ. And there are people who believe God in their hearts, and to them it is counted as righteousness. Not salvation, but righteousness. They can also receive miracles.

But to the unbeliever I say, why be content with a glass of milk, when you can have the cow? Or why fill you up momentarily with a morsel of bread, when you can own the bakery? I mean, why to be content with one miracle, when you can have the Miracle Doer, and enjoy His everlasting blessings?

Great miracles happen because of faith. Faith is to believe, to hope, to put your trust in someone or something. In Genesis chapter 11, we have the story of people who were trying to reach God by building a ladder that could reach to heaven. And they were succeeding.

So much, that God saw what they were doing and confused their language and dispersed them throughout the world, lest they accomplish their purpose. They had faith in what they were doing. Their corporate faith was working. They had the right purpose, but the wrong method. But they put their faith together, and almost accomplished their purpose.

I believe that other than those who are living a committed life to God, who I am persuaded will experience *at least* one miracle from God in their lives, there are a minimum of at least three other kinds of people who *could* receive miracles:

1. People whose faith has been shaken

When Peter walked on water, it was not because he was *holier* than the other disciples. It was because at that time, on the contrary, his faith had been momentarily shaken.

Jesus had finished feeding thousands of people; His disciples were with Him. After He fed the multitudes, Jesus asked the disciples to get in the boat and go before Him to the other side, while He sent the multitudes away. Then, He went to the mountain to pray.

It was now evening, and the boat was in the middle of the sea, being tossed by the waves. It was between 03:00 and 06:00 in the morning when Jesus came to them, walking on the sea.

When they saw Him they were afraid, and thought He was a ghost. Their faith was really shaken! Even Peter, the "Head Elder" was troubled, and doubted: *"Lord, if it's You,* command me to come to You on the water" (Matt. 14:22-28, NKJ).

Peter did not recognize the Lord because he was afraid. Fear can shake your faith and blur your vision. And when your faith has been shaken, something greater must happen to restore your faith: a **miracle!**

2. People who walk by sight and not by faith

Thomas was one of Jesus' disciples. He walked with Him, ate with Him, and heard the Gospel from Him; he knew Him. Yet, he did not believe Jesus when He said that He would resurrect.

When Jesus appeared to the disciples the first time after His resurrection, Thomas was not with them. When the disciples told him about Jesus' appearance, Thomas did not believe, and asked for proof: when you don't meet with Jesus, you can miss the *revelation* of Him.

"Unless I see in His hands the print of the nails, and put my finger into the print of the nails, and put my hand into His side, I will not believe" (John 20:25b, NKJ).

Eight days later, Jesus appeared to the disciples again. This time, Thomas was with them. Jesus told Thomas:

"Reach your finger here, and look at my hands; and reach your hand here, and put it into my side. Do not be unbelieving, but believing."

And Thomas answered and said to Him: "My Lord and my God...!"

Jesus said to him: "Thomas, because you have seen me, you have believed. Blessed are those who have not seen and yet have believed" (John 20:27-29, NKJ).

Sometimes a miracle is necessary to develop faith in the hearts of those who walk by sight and not by faith; even Christians. Not all Christians *know* God. With God, it's a matter of faith! "Faith is the substance of things hoped for, the evidence of things not seen" (Heb.11:1, NKJ).

3. People who have exhausted all their resources

There was a woman who had been sick for twelve years, and *had spent all her living on physicians*, but could not be healed. This woman came from behind and touched Jesus' garments when He was on his way to raise a young woman who died; immediately after touching Him, she was healed of her sickness. (Luke 8:41-44). There is nothing impossible for God.

God will not always be your last resource, but your only and best resource. When it seems that nothing else will work, if you trust God, He will work it out for you. And the best thing is that when He works it out, it is forever!

It would be so wonderful if we always went to Him first, but we do not always have the faith to believe and trust that He can do it. Oh, ye of little faith! But He is always there for us, even when we go to Him last.

This woman came to Jesus after she had spent all her resources. She had not been able to see Jesus before. For twelve years she lived a life of pain, and now was without money.

But the moment she heard about Jesus, and saw Him, she didn't care what the people would say about her. She only knew that Jesus could heal her, and she was going to take the chance, no matter what. After all, she had done all she could. That's how our faith should be; unquenchable! If we have faith as a mustard seed, we will move mountains.

JESUS, THE TRUE LIFE

Once, speaking to His disciples, encouraging their hearts and preparing them for His upcoming death and resurrection, Jesus told them that He was going to prepare a place for them in heaven, with the Father. He told them that they knew where He was going, and the way to get there. Thomas, who later would not believe in His resurrection, said to Him:

"Lord, we do not know where you are going, and how can we know the way?" Jesus said to him, "I am the way, the truth and the life. No one comes to the Father except through me." (John 14:1-6, NKJ).

For the believer, Jesus is life; the source of true and eternal life. Nothing that was created came to exist without Him. He has *been* since the *beginning* with God, and is God Himself. All that is, has been created through Him, by Him and for Him,

"In the beginning *was* the Word, and the Word was *with* God, and the Word *was* God. He *was* in the beginning with God. All things were made through Him, and without Him nothing was made that was made" (John 1:1-3, NKJ). (Also, read John 14:9; 15:23-24; and 17:21-24). This is one of the greatest miracles and mysteries of God; it takes faith for anyone to believe it

Fresh faith, one of the catalysts for miracles

Miracles do not happen by prayer alone. Prayer is an important element for miracles, but prayer without faith; that is, fresh faith, does not work. What do I mean by fresh faith?

Well, I remember when I became a Christian. Man, I thought I was Superman! I believed then that I could change the course of rivers only by speaking it, and that I was faster than a speeding bullet.

I believed I could stop a rushing locomotive with my hands, and that I could bend a bar of steel; so I believed! Sounds like *Clark Kent*, doesn't it? All I want to say is that when you first meet God and God meets you, it seems that nothing is impossible for you.

It is like Clark Kent and Superman. They are one and the same. However, it is only when the timid Clark goes into the booth, changes clothes and transform into the bold man of steel that things really happen. It is then that the faith and boldness of timid Clark changes things around. It is the same thing with us. When we walk in faith and believe, miracles will happen.

I remember one day in Korea, 1981, while serving in the military; it was my first year as a true Christian, and boy, God was working through me! A Sunday worship service had just ended in one of the military chapels in Yong-San, Seoul. I was ready to attend another service nearby, but it was raining "cats and dogs." I mean, it was pouring!

Back then I attended every service possible. That's how strong my faith was; it was fresh faith! I looked around, as if by looking the rain would stop. Really, I was only looking for a witness to a miracle; I *knew* God would stop the rain, only because I wanted to go to the other side and meet Him, and I believed He could do it.

I saw a man leaning against one of the pillars of the chapel, waiting for the rain to stop. I approached the man and asked him if he remembered in the Bible, in 1 Kings, when the Prophet Elijah, by prayer, faith and a word of God, closed the heavens that it did not rain for three years (1 Kg. 17:1).

The man looked at me and answered, "Yes, I remember."

I told him, "Well, I believe by the word of God it's going to stop raining, because I want to attend another service." He looked at me again, saying nothing. Then, looking straight at him, I said, "By the word of God, it's going to stop raining."

The very moment I spoke that short prayer, it stopped raining! I *knew* it was going to happen. I *believed;* I had fresh faith; I spoke things into existence. You see, nothing happens until you speak it into existence, with faith.

"What did I tell you?"

He looked at me again, popped a cigarette in his mouth, fired it up, and began walking. Now, he was walking on my miracle! I thanked God, and I went up to the service. That's fresh faith!

On another occasion, I was in the motor pool checking on soldiers, encouraging them. I was a chaplain assistant in the Army, and my chaplains gave me the *green* light to visit and *minister* with soldiers while they worked. Soldiers in my company called me *The Preacher*.

While working in the motor pool, they were listening to music on the radio. Suddenly, down in the studio, the record playing at the time got stuck, and the song was repeating itself over and over again. The soldiers were getting impatient, mad, and the devil came in; they began to swear.

I jumped in: "Hey, that's not the way; calm down. All you have to do is to have faith in God." I tapped the radio, and immediately the record began playing normally. Of course, they asked me how I did it. "If I have told you once, I have told you twice. It's not me, but the power of God in me. If you believe in God as I have told you, these things will happen to you, too." Again, I believed; I had faith, and it happened!

To them, even those *small* wonders might have seemed impossible, because they did not have the *God* kind of faith. But to me, those things [then] were normal; I called them *miracles*.

It is said that when the Gospel was first introduced in countries like Bangladesh and Indonesia, miracles happened; dead people came back to life; deaf people heard again; the lame walked. Why? Because those new converts believed on the Bible *literally*, as it was written; they had fresh faith! If the Bible said people could come back from the dead, they believed it; literally, without reasoning. And miracles happened.

All things are possible for those who *believe*. But, like with any other thing, faith can get *old* sometimes. How does faith get old? Because of *knowledge*; we substitute faith for knowledge, and with knowledge comes doubt and unbelief in the Word of God. Suddenly, technology and new knowledge in medicine takes the place of faith. Now, I'm not saying medicine is not good; no.

When I get sick, I pray and I go to the doctor. I believe that medicine is a miracle from God. All medicine comes from God's creation: plants, animals, etc. But God also put intelligence in man, the ability to use God's resources for the good of mankind. We were created by Him, in His own image and likeness, so we are intelligent, as He is.

Even Elijah's faith got old! The same Elijah who closed the heavens by a word of God (1 Kg. 17:1-7) that there was no rain for three years, and then brought rain again by the same word of God (1 Kg. 18:41-45); the same Elijah who brought fire from heaven and consumed 450 prophets of Baal, was the same Elijah who ran and hid from Jezebel.

She threatened to kill him, enraged with anger because of the prophets' deaths. That mighty man of God got weary, terrified; his faith got old very quickly in the face of danger (1 Kg. 19:1-4).

No miracle in the Bible ever happened because of people's prayer *only*; they happened because of people's *faith*, mixed with prayer and the will of God. And again:

"Abraham *believed* God and it was accounted to him for righteousness. And he was called the friend of God" (Ja. 2:23, NKJ).

When Peter and John healed the man at the gate of the temple called Beautiful, they did not pray; they were on their way to the temple to pray, but they did not get there until after God healed the man by their hands. They *believed* and *spoke* the healing into existence in the name of Jesus because of their faith and the man's faith (Acts 3:1-6; *16):

"*And His name, through *faith* in His name, has made this man strong, whom you see and know. Yes, the *faith* which comes through Him has given him this perfect soundness in the presence of you all."

****

At the time of Christ's resurrection, the persecution of the church had increased. With Christ no longer physically in the picture, Rome took counsel against Christianity. Herod the king began killing Christians. He killed James the brother of John, and when he saw that his act pleased the Jews, he put Peter in jail (Acts 12:1-2).

Now, the Bible says that prayer was made without ceasing of the church unto God for him. And one night, as Peter was sleeping between two soldiers, bound with chains, the Lord sent an angel to set him free. The angel smote Peter on the side and raised him up. His chains fell off from his hands, and the angel ordered Peter to follow him. Peter thought he was having a vision.

But when they passed the first and second wards, and came unto the Iron Gate that leads to the city, Peter came to *himself* and knew that the Lord had miraculously sent an angel to deliver him from the hands of Herod and the Jews. He came to the house of Mary, the mother of John, where the Christians had gathered to pray for him.

When he knocked at the door, a girl named Rhoda answered. When she recognized Peter's voice, she was so glad he was alive that she did not open the door, but ran inside with the good news.

When they heard her, they did not believe her and told her that she was crazy. But she kept on insisting it was Peter, so they told her it was his *angel*. Peter continued knocking at the door, and when they opened it and saw Peter, they were amazed, still in unbelief. Peter signaled them to be quiet, and began telling them how the Lord had brought him out of prison. (Acts 12:1-17.)

Two points jumped to mind when I read these passages. I know that many will not agree with me in these two points, and that's okay. I'm not claiming to be right; I just think this to be the case.

Number one, although the Bible says that they were praying for him (v.5), I don't think they really believed that Peter was going to leave jail alive. How did I come to this conclusion?

Well, when Peter came to the door, they did not believe it was him. More than that, they thought it was his *angel* (v. 15). If they were praying for his freedom, why didn't they believe when they saw him?

If you believe when you pray, you will have what you ask for (Mk. 11:24); not necessarily miracles, but whatever you pray for, if it is in agreement with the will of God. We must always ask for God's will to be done.

Maybe His will for you at the time that you pray is not a miracle, but a relationship with him; or forgiveness, or faith;

or anything else you may not think you need, but He knows you need.

Secondly, I believe that this miracle happened because of Peter's faith, rather than because of the people's prayer. The Bible says "the *effective, fervent* prayer of a righteous man avails much" (Ja.5:16b, NKJ).

Effective has to do with the active operation of working of *power* and the results of it. James says that faith without works is dead. It was impossible for me to see the effective works of the prayer of the saints who were praying for Peter, simply because they did not believe when they saw him.

They did not have faith in what they prayed for. If they prayed and *believed*, they should not have been surprised when he showed up; rather, they should have been surprised if he didn't show up!

Peter was a righteous man. He was sleeping when the angel came. And I believe that he was sleeping because the peace of God was with him.

I believe Peter's relationship with Christ at this time was so strong that he didn't fear death. He had the peace of God, like Paul, knowing that for him to live was Christ, and to die was *gain*. (Phil. 1:21) He was not looking to die, but he was looking for God, and was not afraid.

He knew God was able to deliver him if He chose to (Dan. 3:17-18). The Bible did not give the indication that Peter prayed, although as a Jew and a Christian, it was customary to pray; he was sleeping in peace, because he had fresh faith! That's why he was able to sleep at such a time, because of the peace of God was in him; he trusted Jesus.

How many of us, honestly, could sleep in a time like this, knowing that the same fate that Peter was facing could be our fate? Only one full of God's presence!

Peter was having a vision (v. 9). When he came to himself, and found himself walking out of prison, with the angel ahead of him, he realized that it was no longer a vision; he was not sleeping. The Lord sent an angel to set him free; it was a miracle!

Don't let your faith get old. Keep it fresh by exercising it daily, by keeping your eyes on God and not on the circumstances, believing that with God all things are possible; then you will see miracles. Peter kept his faith fresh, even in prison.

Without faith, it is impossible to please Him. Faith, the God kind of faith, is a miracle in itself, for not all have *that* kind of faith. All men have faith, but not all have *that* kind of faith. Paul says:

"And that we may be delivered from unreasonable and wicked men: for not all have faith," (2 Thess. 3:2, NKJ) meaning that wicked men don't have the *God kind* of faith, the faith that moves *mountains*. They have faith, but not God's *kind* of faith. They walk disorderly, with no respect for order and law. All men have faith [because all believe in something].

"For I say, through the grace given unto me, to every man that is among you, not to think of himself more highly than he ought to think; but to think soberly, according as God has dealt to *every* man *the* measure of faith." (Ro. 12:3, NKJ.)

But not all have *the God kind of faith*. This book is about miracles, geared to stir up the God *kind* of faith that is in you, because you love Him, and He loves you.

HINDRANCES TO MIRACLES

There are two major hindrances to miracles:

$\left(1\right)$ **-Unbelief/doubt:** "If anyone lacks wisdom, let him ask of God, who gives to all liberally and without reproach, and it will be given to him. But let him ask in faith, with no doubting, for he who doubts is like a wave of the sea driven and tossed by the wind. For let not that man suppose that he will receive anything from the Lord; he is a double minded man, unstable in all his ways" (Ja. 1:5-7, NKJ).

If you are unstable, you are not firm on your belief. And if you are not firm, you can't hold to anything. James also says that faith without works is dead. Likewise, prayer without faith is dead. And:

"Therefore I say unto you, whatsoever things you ask when you pray, *believe* that you receive them, and you will have them;" (Mk. 11:24, NKJ) if you *believe*. That's the key for your miracle: ***believe!***

You must have conviction, confidence, and trust; total reliance in God and His will for your life. If you believe, all things [in God's will] are possible.

(2) – **Un-forgiveness:** A heart that cannot forgive cannot offer any gift to God, not even prayer; neither can it be forgiven by God:

"Therefore, if you bring your gift to the altar, and there remember that your brother has something against you, leave your gift there before the altar, and go your way. First be reconciled to your brother, and then come and offer your gift" (Matt. 5:23-24, NKJ).

And keep in mind that as a Christian, it will require a greater faith to forgive in this instance, because the offense was against you. Forgiveness on your part, when you are the victim, requires true faith and the love of God.

God will not hear or receive anything from you until you have forgiven, until your heart is at peace with your *brother*. Who is your brother? Your brother can be your neighbor…or your **enemy!**

"And whenever you stand praying, if you have anything against anyone, forgive him that your Father who is in heaven may also forgive you your trespasses. But if you do not forgive, neither will your Father in heaven forgive your trespasses" (Mk. 11:25, NKJ). And if God doesn't forgive you, neither will He hear you.

The miracle at Lourdes

On February 11, 1858, Catholic history says that the Virgin Mary appeared to Bernadette Soubirous in the grotto of Massabielle, Lourdes, in the foothills of the French Pyrenees, France.

As a *born again* Christian, I do not believe the Virgin Mary really appeared to those girls in France; but that's *my* faith. I believe that only Jesus and His angels have the power of miraculous appearance, known as a Christophany or Theophany.

Now, I'm not saying that Catholics are not Christians. I was raised in the Catholic Church for the first twenty-five years of my life and I learned good moral principles, and experienced some of the most giving hearts one can ever see, and I knew Jesus Christ as my Savior and Lord.

But I also "learned" other "doctrines" germane only to the Catholic Church, not biblically founded; like praying to Mary and the "Catholic" saints, or to place Mary as mediator between Jesus and man. The Bible clearly states that there is only one God, and one mediator between God and men, the man Christ Jesus (1Tim. 2:5).

But I'm saying that as Catholics, as well as other denominations, we need to get the true revelation of Jesus Christ; we have to be *born again*.

Born again Christians should not place any other biblical entity in the same divine level of Jesus, with the same power and authority. That's not biblically founded:

"You shall have no other gods before me. You shall not make unto you any graven image, or any likeness of *anything* that is in heaven above, or that is in the earth beneath, or that is in the water under the earth; you shall not bow yourself to them, nor serve them:

'for I the Lord your God am a jealous God, visiting the iniquity of the fathers upon the children unto the third generation of them that hate me, and showing mercy unto thousands of them that love me, and keep my commandments" (Ex. 20:3-6). Jesus was the only one miraculously *conceived* by the Holy Spirit; He is God.

But the important thing here is how God can use whatever happened, or didn't happen in Lourdes to miraculously change people's lives forever.

And that's the real miracle; that people's lives are changed forever simply because of faith in Jesus. God can use anything or anybody to perform a miracle for you, if you believe.

If God can set a bush on fire and not consume it just to call the attention of one man to fulfill His purpose (Gen. 3:2), He can certainly use a little girl's faith to change the lives of many. Just think of the many lives that were changed for the better by God through this girl, because of her faith. That's the miracle!

*****

Franz Werfel was a Jewish writer living in Vienna in Hitler's time. Werfel was an outspoken Anti-Nazi. He left Vienna in 1940 with his wife, running from Hitler. They tried to make it to the United States via Spain and Portugal.

With no visas or passports, it was difficult and dangerous. Had they been caught, in all probability they would have been taken to a concentration camp and killed, with other Jews; but they made it to Lourdes, France.

Not a very religious man, Werfel found himself doing something he was not accustomed to: he prayed. Not only did he pray, but he *believed* that he could make it to America. It was not only his prayer, for he was not a very religious man, but it was his newfound faith, coupled with prayer, that *moved his mountain.*

Right at the foot of the Spring of Lourdes, he drank the water of the famous spring, believed by many to have healing powers, and there he believed for a miracle. Think it not strange that people believed there was healing power on those waters.

The Bible speaks about people bringing sick folk to Peter, so that Peter's shadow might overshadow and heal them (Acts 5:15). But it was God working miracles by Peter, and not Peter's shadow healing people. Peter's shadow could heal no one. .Peter's shadow was only God's conduit to perform the miracles (Acts 5:15). People had faith in the God Peter served.

The Bible also speaks about people being healed when handkerchiefs and aprons that had touched the body of Paul were placed on them, and their diseases departed from them, and the evil spirits went out of them (Acts 19:12). The same happened with the waters of Lourdes.

It was not the handkerchiefs, or the aprons that healed them. It was God working special miracles by the hand of Paul (Acts 19:11). These items were only God's channel to lift people's faith, and to perform miracles.

Well, helped by Vivian Fry, an American Quaker in a mission to France to save artists from Hitler, Werfel made it to America. Isn't it *miraculous,* that God always has someone to bring your prayer to come to pass?

God always has a *ram* in the bush for you. He didn't promise providence, but protection. This miracle happened because God wanted a Jew to testify about Him, about His miraculous power. All miracles happen for the glory of God, and not for the glory of man. Man has no glory outside of God.

Werfel made it to Los Angeles, CA, and that's how the *Song of Bernadette* was born, in the streets of LA, by a man saved from death by a miracle through faith. It was the love of God, coupled with the fourteen-year-old poor girl's faith, the miracle that saved his life. That little girl's miracle kept his faith alive!

This book is about the supernatural world of miracles; a world that can only be believed and lived by those with the mustard seed kind of faith, and by those who have experienced a miracle in their own lives, and by those who need a miracle, Christians or no Christians, but know that God is real.

I believe that at one time or another, we who believe in the God of creation will experience a miracle; even if a small miracle. However, some of us may never be aware of that miracle. *Your very own life is a miracle!*

MODERN DAY MIRACLES

In the "Yahoo" news of February 28, 2008, an article recounts the story of an Irish man who recovered his sight after two years of total blindness. Bob McNichol was blinded two years before in a freak accident, when red-hot liquid aluminum exploded at a re-cycling business in November 2005.

After doctors gave up hope on restoring his sight, he heard a *miracle* operation called Osteo-Odonto-Keratoprosthesis [OOKP], performed at the Sussex Eye Hospital in Brighton, England, by Dr. Christopher Liu. Now, here is my fascination about the procedure. It involves creating a support for an artificial cornea from the patient's own tooth and the surrounding bone, or from a compatible match.

Bob's son, Robert, age twenty-three, donated a tooth, its root and part of the jaw; good son, wasn't he? McNichol's right eye socket was rebuilt, part of Robert's tooth was inserted, a hole was drilled, and a lens was inserted in the tooth.

The first operation lasted ten agonizing hours, and a second operation lasted five hours. But at the end, he recovered enough sight to "get around" and watch television.

"I have come out from complete darkness to be able to do simple things," said McNichol.

Now, who would not say this was indeed a miracle from God? Who would think a tooth can help someone to recover the vision? *Miracles*, acts we cannot explain, continue to happen; even today!

*****

On New Year's Day in 2001, Philip McCord, director of facilities management for the Sisters of Providence of Saint Mary-of-the Woods, entered the Immaculate Conception Church in Indianapolis to pray.

Mr. McCord was trying to make up his mind about having a cornea transplant on his right eye. A short time earlier, he had surgery to remove a cataract from his eye. After the surgery, he experienced heaviness and could not see through the eye.

A specialist in Indianapolis recommended that the cornea be removed and replaced with one from an organ donor. The operation had a 60 percent chance of success, with a recovery period of two years, and Mr. McCord was unsure about having the surgery; he came almost to the point of canceling the surgery.

One day, in his search for answers, he decided to come to a church and pray about it. He was not a devout Christian, although he had been raised under the American Baptist Church.

He went to that church, thinking that a prayer could not hurt. He was a person used to taking care of his own business, but this one was a little heavy for him, so he told God that he needed help getting through this. He did not pray for a miracle, but for guidance and reassurance from God. After his prayer, he went on his way. When he left the church, he felt much better.

"Maybe there's something to this thing of prayer after all; it worked. I can have my surgery now."

The next day, when he woke up, the heaviness and swelling on his right eye had receded, although he still could not see out of his eye. Some weeks later, he returned to see the eye specialist with the intention of setting a date for the surgery. After he told the doctor he felt better, the doctor proceeded to examine the eye with an ocular microscope.

"It was really kind of funny," McCord said. "He looked at my eye... and looked at my chart, and said, 'Hum!' Now, I had worked in health care for a long time, and when a doctor says, 'Hum,' [it means something]."

The specialist asked him if his local physician had done anything, to which McCord answered no. When the specialist asked McCord if he had done anything, McCord replied that he had said a prayer.

The doctor acknowledged that the eye's condition had improved vastly. The specialist came to the conclusion that since the swelling had been removed, the lack of vision could be corrected with a very ordinary laser treatment.

The laser treatment took place some days later. McCord now had 20/20 vision in both eyes! God had performed a miracle for a man who did not pray for a miracle; he prayed for guidance, but God gave him what he needed!

Super spiritual people may think that God will not act on a petition like this. However, I'm of the persuasion that God looks at the heart and faith of people. This man only knew that there was peace and strength in God.

He came looking for strength, and instead received a miracle; he had faith as a mustard seed. God saw his faith and his heart, and healed him! We too can receive miracles, if we humble ourselves before God, and have a right and pure heart. Like a song says:

"Who can ascend to the hills of the Lord, but he that has clean hands and a pure heart?" *(http://www.freerepublic.com/focus/freligion/1757399/posts).

(*Note: The information about this miracle can no longer be found on the website but if you Google it, you'll find various sites that recorded Mr. McCord's miracle).

CHRONOLOGY

Nothing has fascinated the minds of people more than the mystery of miracles, second only to the birth, death and resurrection of Jesus Christ, which are considered by most the greatest miracles of all.

But when we talk about the miracles of the birth, death, and resurrection of Jesus Christ, they stand alone also as the greatest *events* in the history of mankind.

The birth, death and resurrection of Jesus Christ are an exception to the rule of miracles. They are not great acts of God, but they are the greatest prophecies and promises ever from God. Miracles are divine works of God, unknown until they happen.

But these events were announced and expected (Isaiah 9:6; Psalm 22; Luke 1:26-33; Luke 9:21-22; Mk. 8:31). The birth, death and especially His resurrection, were the greatest catalysts for change in the history of mankind.

These events together changed the lives of everyone thereafter, believers and non- believers. After Christ's birth, history took on a new meaning.

The Dating of History

For centuries, man tried to date historical events by historical figures, names or events, unsuccessfully. People either hated or loved them. And once these figures died, or the events were passed, they were gone from history.

But in the year 532 A.D., all that changed. A monk by the name of Dyonisius Exiguus began a Christian system of dating events that solved the situation once and forever.

Jesus Christ is someone who, although hated by some and loved by many, has fascinated the minds of all, believers and non-believers. Everyone talks about Christ; out of love or out of hate. No one else has influenced the world as Jesus has. What did Dyonisius do?

He dated all the events before Christ's birth as B.C. (before Christ), and the events after Christ's birth as A.D. (anno Domini, Latin for *in the year of our Lord*).

For example, something that happened in 300 A.D. occurred 300 hundred years after the birth of Jesus. An event 100 B.C. happened 100 years before Christ's birth. That to me is a miracle in itself!

But before we can go any further, I believe it is fair to establish the authenticity of Jesus Christ as seen through the eyes of non-Christians, historians and organizations, so Jesus would not become a symbol for Christians only, but a symbol for the entire human race, as He indeed is.

Josephus

Josephus was a Jewish historian who lived from 37 A.D. until approximately 100 A.D. He was a member of the priestly aristocracy of the Jews, and was taken hostage by the Roman Empire in the great Jewish revolt of 66-70 A.D.

He spent the rest of his life in or around Rome as an advisor and historian to three emperors: Vespasian, Titus and Domitian:

"For centuries, the works of Josephus were more widely read in Europe than any books other than the Bible. They are invaluable sources of eyewitness testimony to the development of Western civilization, including the foundation and growth of Christianity in the 1st Century." (http://www.josephus-I.com).

'Josephus mentions New Testament events and people in some of his works. For many skeptics, this is viewed as significant evidence against the myth and legend theories that plagued early Christianity. Here are some excerpts of his view:

"Now there about this time Jesus, a wise man, if it be lawful to call him a man; for he was a doer of wonderful works, a teacher of such men as receive the truth with pleasure. He drew over to him both many of the Jews and many of the Gentiles. He was [the] Christ.

And when Pilate, at the suggestion of the principal men amongst us, had condemned him to the cross, those that loved him at the first did not forsake him; for he appeared to them alive again the third day; as the divine prophets had foretold these and ten thousand other wonderful things concerning him. And the tribes of Christians, so named from him, are not extinct at this day." (Antiques, Book 18, chapter 3, paragraph 3.) (http://www.josephus-I.com).

Thallus

A Jewish writer of Mediterranean history, during the middle of the first century, Thallus also mentioned Jesus in his writings. One his existent fragments relates the night of the crucifixion:

"On the whole world there pressed a most fearful darkness; and the rocks were rent by an earthquake, and many places in Judea and other districts were thrown down." This passage consists with the writings in the Gospel of Matthew, Chapter 27:45-51.

Justin Martyr

Justin Martyr was a second century philosopher and theologian born of pagan parents. He later converted to Christianity, and was executed during the reign of Emperor Marcus Aurellious for refusing to offer sacrifices to the pagan gods.

He wrote that the events of Christ's crucifixion could be validated by the report of Pontius Pilate. (http://raptureforums.com.) Pontius Pilate also recorded the events of the crucifixion of Christ.

Pliny the Younger

Pliny was a Roman author who at one time served as governor of Bithynia in Asia Minor. He was concerned about the rapid growth of Christianity and its potential for threatening the beliefs of Rome.

Because of this, he wrote the emperor to explain how he interrogated those he believed were Christians. Pliny related that if those he interrogated would not worship the emperor, he would have them executed. In some cases, he would torture them to gather information about the emerging Christian movement.

In one of such cases, he tortured two deaconesses and wrote to the emperor concerning the information he had gathered. He wrote how these Christians gathered on a fixed day before it was light, and sang in alternate verses of a hymn to Christ. (The Tenth Book of Pliny's Letters) (http://www.raptureforums.com.)

There is testimony of at least a dozen other non-Christian historians and organizations: Roman, Greek, and Jews that wrote about Jesus' life, the most notable being Cornelius Tacitus, Suetonious Tranquillas, Phlegon, Lucian Samosata, The Jewish Talmud, and the Babylonian Talmud, validating the authenticity of Christ, making Jesus not only a Christian figure, but a universal figure. Jesus was indeed the *Miracle Maker*, as Josephus had identified Him.

MORE ABOUT MIRACLES

What are miracles? Miracles are those supernatural acts that defy one or more natural laws, and yet are believable because they have a source: *God*. Miracles are those acts that can only be explained by faith through the intervention of God.

Faith is *one* catalyst for miracles. Without faith it is impossible to please God. Faith is the substance of things hoped for, the evidence of things not seen (Heb. 11:6). The Message Bible puts it in an even more practical, easier to understand text:

"The fundamental fact of existence is that this *trust* in God, this *faith,* is the firm foundation under everything that makes life worth living."

Faith is the ability to call those things that are not, as though they were. It was by faith that the worlds were framed by the word of God, so that things which are seen were not made of things which are visible (Heb. 11:3). Again, the Message Bible helps us to understand:

"By faith, we see the world called into existence by God's word; what we see, created by who we don't see."

It cannot be simpler to understand. In other words, the creation, *life, did not come from matter,* but from the word of God, something real but invisible, tangible only through faith, so that man will not boast on himself.

Matter, then, came from life; the Zoe kind of life. We at times are at much loss, simply because we are satisfied with what man says, instead of searching the word of God to find the real truth about things:

"You search the Scriptures, because in them you think you have eternal life, and these are they that testify of me. But you are not willing to come to me that you may have life" (John 5:39, NKJ). It is only in God that we can find the beginning, the source of life, which is God Himself.

The New Testament alone contains more than fifty miracles. A great number of miracles occurred also in the Old Testament. Together, we have an array of undeniable wonders of God to explore. Which was the greatest miracle of all?

In a moment, we'll study some of these miracles. I will not try to rationalize these wonders, but will simply present them, by faith, for you to consider.

We may never agree on the greatness of these miracles, simply because each one of us will see miracles based on our own experience, need, or level of faith. I can only attempt to challenge you to *choose* the greatest miracle of all to you, according to your faith. Now, let's travel through the marvelous world of miracles in the Bible.

Miracles in the Old Testament

Although I would like to emphasize the miracles of the New Testament, mostly because of their relativity to Jesus Christ, it would be an injustice not to see the *evolution* of the miracles of God. As people changed their view of God, so the miracles changed in nature.

Creation, the First Miracle of God

Genesis is the book of beginnings, where God created the heavens and the earth with order and structure, and all life: human, animal, and plant life. It is also in Genesis that God established the first human institution: the family, with the creation of Adam and Eve, the first humans on earth, and their relationship with God and their own children, Cain and Abel, and later on with Seth, their third son.

Genesis first established God as the *beginning* of all things; not a *created* God, but a God that simply *was* [and is] *the* beginning, the Creator, with the progressive revelation of Christ as God:

"*In the beginning, God...*" (Gen. 1:1.); "In the beginning *was* the word, and the word *was* with God, and the word *was* God; the same *was in* the *beginning* with God" (John 1:1-2, NKJ). God was the Creator, not created; He is *Creation*. And then He began the sub-process of creation (Gen. 1:1(b), until He created *Man*, His masterpiece:

"Let *Us* make man in *Our* image, according to *Our* likeness; let *them* have dominium over the fish of the sea, over the birds of the air, and over the cattle, over all the earth and over every creeping thing that creeps on the earth" (Gen. 1:26, NKJ.)

Life began with God; *all life;* "And the Lord God formed man of the dust of the ground, and breathed into his nostrils the breath of life: and man became a living soul" (Gen. 2:7, NKJ).

The Nile and Egypt's Waters Turn into Blood

After Joseph died in the land of Goshen, Egypt, another king (a Pharaoh), who did not know Joseph, raised to power in Egypt. This king was cruel, and for fear of the growth in number of the people of Israel, decided to make slaves of Israel.

After God spoke to Moses in the burning bush (Exodus 3), He sent him with a demand to Pharaoh, to "let His people go" from their 400 years of bondage and forced labor. In Exodus Chapter 7:19-22, God commanded Moses and Aaron to strike the waters of Egypt,

"Then the Lord spoke to Moses, 'Say to Aaron, "Take your rod and stretch out your hand over the waters of Egypt, over their streams, over their rivers, over their ponds, and over all their pools of water, that they may become blood.'"

"And there shall be blood throughout all the land of Egypt, both in *buckets* of wood and *pitchers* of stone. And Moses and Aaron did so, just as the Lord commanded. So he lifted up the rod and struck the waters that were in the river, in the sight of Pharaoh and in the sight of his servants. And all the waters that were in the river were turned to blood."

Some scholars argue that this verse (vs. 20) means that the waters of the Nile have been polluted with fine red earth that God had spread out through heavy flooding. However, if it was so, the red earth was there before God commanded Moses to turn the waters into blood. And, if the red sand was there as "they" said, it was placed by God, according to their own admission (the scholars).

How come the fish and the life that was in the rivers and waters did not die until Moses turned the water into blood? And, when have we seen fish dying because of red earth?

The Egyptians were able to drink the waters before the miracle, and ate the fish from the river, with red earth in it. How come they could not drink the waters after Moses and Aaron stretched the rod over the river?

The waters turned into blood, no doubt about it. But to me, one thing that disqualifies this miracle as the greatest miracle is that Pharaoh's magicians were able to duplicate this miracle (vs. 22).

Pharaoh ordered his magicians to duplicate the act of Moses and Aaron, causing more sorrow and death to Egypt. It's God using the foolishness of man to confound the world. By challenging the power of God, Pharaoh caused more death to his own people. No one can defy God and win!

Another Miracle: the Frogs

In Exodus Chapter 8, Moses brings frogs over all Egypt. In Egypt, frogs were connected to the goddess of fertility and childbirth, *Heqt*. By this miracle, God showed Pharaoh that

He was in charge of reproduction in the earth, not Pharaoh. Again, Pharaoh's magicians duplicated this miracle, thus multiplying death in Egypt.

With this miracle, God showed that the waters turned into blood was a miracle, because by this time (the frog's miracle), there was life again in the waters, as the Lord determined in Chapter 7, verse 25. Again, the magicians were able to duplicate this miracle, disqualifying it as the greatest miracle of all.

Lice: the Superiority of God's Power

So the Lord said to Moses, "Say to Aaron, 'Stretch out your rod, and strike the dust of the land, so that it may become lice throughout all the land of Egypt,' and they did so; for Aaron stretched out his hand with his rod and struck the dust of the earth, and it became lice on man and beast. All the dust of the land became lice throughout all the land of Egypt" (Ex. Chapter 8:16-19).

This miracle established the superiority of God. Up until then, the magicians had been able to duplicate Moses' miracles; not this time! The magicians could not duplicate this act. They recognized that the *Finger of God* was the cause of the miracles, acknowledging that the Hebrew God was more powerful than the gods of Egypt. Pharaoh's anger grew.

Flies: the Separation of Peoples

This and the next miracles established a unique precedent: the people of God, Israel, were protected, separated from *Egypt*. In the previous plagues, all the land of Egypt was affected. Here, God truly declared to Pharaoh that He was the God over the earth and the God of Israel:

"And in that day I'll set apart the land of Goshen, in which my people dwell, that no swarms of flies shall be there, in order that you may know that I am the Lord in the midst of the land" (Ex. Chapter 8:22, NKJ).

Through this separation, God showed that He was in control, and that He cared for His people. This miracle, although it established God's sovereignty, is not considered the greatest miracle of all, simply because it occurred in a time in which flies were common in the dry, hot climate of Egypt.

There were many more miracles in the Old Testament, all with great significance in the lives of those that experienced them.

But I'd like now to move on to the miracles of the New Testament, simply because of their intimate relation with the Lord Jesus Christ, and because it is here, in the New Testament, that I believe the *greatest miracle of all* is amplified, personified in Jesus Christ.

TABLE OF CONTENTS

Foreword iii
Introduction vii
The Purpose of Miracles 9
Miracles 17
Who May Receive Miracles? 24
Jesus, the True Life 29
Hindrances to Miracles 38
Modern Day Miracles 44
Chronology 48
More About Miracles 53
Angels: Miracles of God 63
Miracles in the New Testament 68
The Greatest Miracle of All 89
Love, the Greatest Miracle of All 91
Unconditional Forgiveness 102
Some Miracles in My Life 113
Postscript 116

ANGELS: MIRACLES OF GOD

Before we deal with the New Testament miracles, allow me to briefly address miracles that the Lord has for us daily:

Angels, in a sense, are miracles. They are extraordinary creatures, *created* by God, with extraordinary power (Ps. 103:20; 2 Kg. 19:20). They appear both in the Old and New Testaments. They are all ministering spirits, sent forth to minister to those who will inherit salvation (Heb.1:14). You don't see them, but they are there!

They are a very well organized structure in the *angelic* realm, and are designated according to their rank. Michael is the prince angel in charge of the angels of war (Dan. 10:13). He is also called an archangel, one who governs over other angels.

Angels do not look the same. They have a variety in their appearance, depending on their responsibility. Gabriel, the messenger angel, has an appearance of a man (Dan.9:21).

Cherubim, the guardian angels (they guard the throne of God), are beautiful, out of the ordinary creatures, covered with precious stones (Ez. 28:13-14), and have four wings.

Seraphim, angels in charge of the worship in heaven have six wings; with two they fly, with two they cover their face, and with the other two wings they cover their feet (Isaiah 6:2).

Every believer has a guardian angel assigned (Ps. 91:11-12), or at least two that cover and protect us with their wings (Psalm 91:4). You don't see them, but they are there!

God has no wings, so the Bible must be referring to angels when it says that God covers us with His *wings*. God is in the business of protecting **us**, and angels are His protecting agents; there are legions of them at His service. Following is a story of angels, as told by a father.

The Birdies – a Story about Guardian Angels

On July 22, 1993, on a business flight to Washington, DC, and while changing planes in Denver, Mr. Lloyd Glenn was asked to see the Customer Representative as soon as possible.

Evidently, Mr. Glenn thought that something wrong had happened at home. When he was finally able to get off the plane, he was told that there had been an emergency at his home. He was able to get to a telephone and called the trauma center of the Mission Hospital, where he was told that his son, Brian, had been trapped, crushed by the automatic doors of the garage, and that when his wife found him, Bryan was clinically dead.

Thankfully to God, a neighbor doctor performed CPR on Brian and the paramedics continued the treatment on their way to the hospital, and by the time Mr. Glenn made the call to the hospital, Brian had been resuscitated and doctors believed he would miraculously live. The question now was to know how much damage had been done to his brain and heart. It would take some time to know and a miracle for Brian not to have suffered any damage.

Six hours after the garage door crushed his son, Mr. Glenn finally made it to the hospital. Seeing his son in the intensive care unit on a respirator, with all the tubes and monitors all over was not easy.

But Brian was alive, so there was still hope. Brian's mother was near Bryan when he arrived at the hospital, and it was very comforting to find a supportive smile in her. Bryan was going to live, and preliminary tests showed that his heart would be okay; two miracles in the same day! How much more could he have asked for?

And the miracles continued. Brian woke up, and there was no neurological or physical harm. His first words were, "Daddy, hold me." You can imagine that those were the most beautiful words any father could ever hear from a son who has challenged and defeated death. It was impossible to measure the impact of his miraculous survival when the story spread all over the hospital.

Brian finally went home, in a midst of joy and gratitude from his parents. The story attests to the unique reverence his parents felt for the life and love that comes to those who have such a close encounter with death, and live.

As the result of Bryan's miracle of life, the entire family's relationship changed. Now, everyone in the family was as close and loving with each other as never before.

God's Possibility to Man's Impossibility

A month later to the day of the accident, one afternoon, Brian awoke from his nap and called his parents to sit down near him, because he had a story to tell. They were surprised to hear Bryan talking long sentences, for he usually spoke only in small phrases. Following is Bryan's story as told by Mr. Lloyd:

"Do you remember when I got stuck under the garage door? Well, it was so heavy and it hurt really *bad*. I called to you, but you couldn't hear me. I started to cry, but then it hurt too *bad*. And then the *birdies* came."

"The birdies?" my wife asked, puzzled.

"Yes," he replied. "The birdies made a whooshing sound and flew into the garage. They took care of me."

"They did?"

"Yes," he said. "One of the birdies came and got you. She came to tell you I got stuck under the door."

A sweet reverent feeling filled the room. The spirit was so strong and yet lighter than air. My wife realized that a three year-old had no concept of death and spirits, so he was referring to the beings [angels] who came to him from beyond as "birdies" because they were up in the air like birds that fly.

"What did the birdies look like?" she asked.

Brian answered, "They were so beautiful! They were dressed in white; all white. Some of them had green and white. But some of them had just white

"Did they say anything?"

"Yes," he answered. "They told me the baby would be alright."

"The baby?" my wife asked, confused.

And Brian answered, "The baby lying on the garage floor." He went on, "You came out and opened the garage door and ran to the baby. You told the baby to stay and not leave."

My wife nearly collapsed upon hearing this, for she had indeed gone and knelt beside Brian's body, and seeing his crushed chest and unrecognizable features, knowing he was already dead, she looked up around her and whispered, "Don't leave us, Brian, please stay if you can."

As she listened to Brian telling her the words she had spoken, she realized that the spirit had left his body and was looking down from above to his little lifeless form. "Then what happened?" she asked.

"We went on a trip," he said, "far, far away. We flew so fast up in the air. They're so pretty, Mommy," he added. "And there are lots and lots of birdies."

Brian continued with the story. He told that the birdies told him that he had to come back and tell everybody about the birdies. "You have to play baseball and tell everyone about the birdies."

Then the person in the bright light kissed him and waved bye-bye. "Then whoosh, the big sound came and they went into the clouds." (http://www.snpes.com/glurge/birdies.asp).

By this story, one can see that angels are always with us, but at times, God has to open our spiritual eyes that we may see them. In 2 Kings chapter six, the prophet Elisha asked God to open the eyes of the young man traveling with him, so he could see God's army [angels] protecting them. Even when we don't see them, God's angels are always with us.

MIRACLES IN THE NEW TESTAMENT

The Bible is full of miracles, both in the Old and New Testaments. We'll explore some miracles in the New Testament, simply because of their relationship to Jesus Christ. The Gospels alone cover a vast multitude of the miracles of Jesus, His disciples and other believers at the time. The Gospel of Luke alone contains more than twenty miracles.

A Man Healed of Leprosy

Leprosy is a disease that attacks the skin and nerves of an individual. It causes the skin to swell badly and to become lumpy and stained, or tarnished. People fear this disease because it causes people's appearance to change, and not for the good.

Leprosy affects the end of the nerves of the face, arms and legs. It's also feared because it causes loss of feeling, making people vulnerable to injuries or burns because of the loss of feelings, and severe damage to the nerves may cause paralysis. However, it seldom causes death.

Leprosy was common in the time that Jesus walked on this earth. Luke 5:12-14 tells us about a man healed of leprosy by Jesus:

"And it happened when he was in a certain city, that behold, a man who was full of leprosy saw Jesus; and he fell on his face and implored him, saying, Lord, if You are willing, You can make me clean." Then He put His hand and touched him, saying, *'I am willing; be cleansed.'* Immediately the leprosy left him."

Matthew 8:2 has the man *worshipping* Jesus when he came to Him. Three things immediately jump out of this miracle:

(1) – The man approached Jesus *worshipping* Him.

It's so important that we acknowledge the deity of Jesus. It's only when we *receive* Him that we have access to His power. It's only then that we have the power to *become* the sons of God (John 1:12). In the natural, only legitimate sons will inherit their father's inheritance.

Not all the children living in your home are your sons (or daughters). Only by birth or adoption can one become a son [or daughter] (Ro. 8:14-17).

In the United States, particularly, we have the system of foster homes. The government pays you to receive children in your home before adoption. Commonly, these children have been legally taken away from their natural parents, or have lost both of their parents through accidents or other causes, or have been abandoned by their parents.

These children become your *foster* children, legally, but not your sons (or daughters). You receive money for them to stay in your home; you do not place them in your will. You keep them for a while, or until another home is found for them. A son stays in the house forever (John 8:35).

Well, the same happens with God. All of us are His *children* by virtue of creation; He created us. But not all of us are His *sons*. Only by adoption or *spiritual* birth can we become *sons* and heirs of God, and joint-heirs with Christ (Ro. 8:14-17).

Once, speaking to a multitude that had rejected Him, Jesus told them, "You are of your father the devil, and the desires of your father you want to do" (John 8:44, NKJ). A sinful life without repentance, and the rejection of Christ can lead us to lose our inheritance with God.

(2) – This man, although he knew who Jesus was and the power that was in Him, questioned His willingness:

"Lord, if you are willing, You can make me clean." The danger of doubting or questioning the power and deity of Jesus is that of losing our miracles. James clearly states it when he says:

"But let him ask in faith, with no doubting, for he who doubts is like a wave of the sea driven and tossed by the wind. For let not that man suppose that he will receive anything from the Lord; he is a double-minded man, unstable in all his ways" (James 1:6-7, NKJ).

Wavering, doubt, may cause us to lose our miracles. We must always stand fast in faith, and see the salvation of the Lord.

(3) – *Leprosy* is a contagious disease; however, Jesus touched this man with no fear of contamination.

Jesus has no fear of touching us, no matter what kind of condition we are in. There is no disease in the world that He can touch and get infected, no matter how infectious the disease is; He did it once and for all. He took all of our infirmities upon Him. He who had no sin became sin for us. In other words, the One who had no infections in Him became infected for us, that we would not be infected with sin anymore.

Jesus becoming sin for us was a miracle in itself, perhaps the greatest miracle of all. Was it? Talking about the miraculous *touch* of Jesus catapults me to the next miracle:

The Woman with the Issue of Blood

In one occasion, while Jesus was on His way with His disciples to bring a young girl who had died back to life, a woman who was sick touched him, and immediately she was healed:

"And suddenly, a woman who had a flow of blood for twelve years came from behind and touched the hem of His garment, for she said to herself, 'If only I may touch His garment, I should be made well.' But Jesus turned around, and when He saw her, He said,

'Be of good cheer, daughter, your faith has made you well.' And the woman was made well from that hour" (Matt. 9:20-22).

This woman did not pray for the miracle. She just believed and **touched** Jesus. Jesus wants us to touch Him, by faith. This miracle has to be rated well up there in the scale of great miracles.

Some time ago, I was reading about little girls in one of the nations of Africa. These little girls are raped or made to be married and have children at a very young age, some as young as eleven. As a result, many of them develop a discharge of blood that can only be stopped through surgery. Some may be sick for years, discharging blood everywhere they go, becoming a shame in their country; as the woman with the issue of blood became a shame to her country. So, you can imagine how this woman in the Bible felt for twelve long years. Ah, but along came Jesus!

One thing jumps immediately to mind, and that is the faith of this woman. I said previously that faith is the catalyst for miracles. This woman had faith, much faith. She came from behind. She did not pray: she just *believed*, and pushed ahead!

At the time, people with this kind of disease were considered unclean, not to be near *regular* people; but she didn't care. She was determined to get her miracle, and no one was going to stop her from getting it; she knew it would happen, *now!*

She had waited for a long time. She knew that anything *on* Jesus became *Him*, with all His power; even His garments. She only wanted to touch His garments. Oh, that we all had that kind of faith!

Luke gives us an even more dramatic narrative of this event (Luke 8:43-47). In Luke's Gospel, not only His disciples were with Jesus, but a great multitude was thronging and pressing Jesus. Even so, He felt her touch.

When He asked who had touched Him, no one admitted to it. His disciples, skeptical that He felt someone touching Him, asked, "Master, the multitude throng and press You and You say, Who touched Me?'" But Jesus said,

"Someone touched Me, for I perceived power going out from Me."

When you touch Jesus, [virtue] healing power flows out of Him. Jesus has been touching us, or trying to touch us forever. Now, it is time for us to take another approach, and *touch* Him. He wants to release His healing power on us, and the only way to release that power is by us touching Him.

It's like the light bulb. We know that electricity is always flowing through the electrical conduits in your house. But no light will come on by you only looking at the light bulb, or at the switch receptacle. It's not by saying, "Let there be light," that the light will come on. No, you must touch, flip the switch, and then the electricity is activated, released, and the light will come on.

Faith is the switch that releases Jesus' virtue, power, to you. When you release your faith, you are touching Jesus; you are flipping the switch, you are activating the power in Him.

Won't you release your faith today in believing for the miracle that you are looking for? Only be sure that you are not asking amiss, but that you are asking for the right purpose, and not doubting. You'll have your petition; even a miracle, if it's the will of God for your life.

The healing of this woman is not the greatest miracle of all, but a great miracle indeed. Today, thanks to new medical technology and scientific knowledge, doctors are able to cure blood flow diseases like that of the woman. Even the Army has patches that can slow down blood flow. But back then, it was a different story.

The Bible says that this woman spent all her money, and still was not cured. I believe that for her, that was the greatest miracle of all! Let me say here that whatever miracle you are in need of, when it happens, it should be the greatest miracle of all for you, right then.

Feeding the Five Thousand

In the book of Luke, Chapter 9:10-17, we find the miracle of the feeding of the five thousand men with only five loaves of bread and two fish. I believe that there were more than five thousand people there, because it was common for women and children to accompany the men to come and hear Jesus (Matt. 14:21). Yet, it's enough to know that Jesus was able to feed at least five thousand people.

Jesus is the God of multiplication, the God of abundance. When He gives, He gives in good measure, pressed down, shaken together and running over. It was a great miracle, especially when the disciples could not go and purchase the food needed because they were in a desolate place.

The disciples suggested the people go and find towns in the surrounding areas to lodge and find food to eat, but Jesus forbade it, knowing what He was about to do. He was also testing their faith.

One thing that really touched me about this miracle is that in the narrative of Matthew, Jesus not only fed the people, but He moved with *compassion* [love] and healed the sick. When Jesus heals, He heals the entire tri-dimensional person: spirit, soul and body. Jesus does a complete work.

I was talking with Jared, one of my sons after his second day in school, and he was explaining the definitions of health and wellness to me.

Wellness is the process of being in good health, while health is to be completely well mentally, physically, and spiritually. In other words, to be healthy you must be balanced in all three areas of your being. Jesus not only begins the process of wellness in you, but when He finishes with you, you are in complete health!

Again, although a great miracle, I do not consider this the greatest miracle; simply because in modern times we are able to, in just hours, put together tons of food to feed not only five thousand, but thousands of thousands of people at once.

Food distribution to victims of national disasters and wars is a prime example. I believe that for these people, to have their hunger satisfied right there and then, when they needed it, was the greatest miracle of all.

There have been many great miracles, both in the New and Old Testaments, each one equally important to every person involved. The blind seeing, the lame walking, demons cast out from people; but as great at these miracles were, they were not the greatest miracles of all. Not by my definition.

Today, science is so advanced that people receiving artificial prostheses, and getting new *hands* is very common. Some years ago a hand was transplanted from a dead person to a living one.

Just recently, while watching television, I saw the attachment of the first *bionic* complete arm, from shoulder to hand, put on a woman; a fully working hand that responds to electronic impulses from the brain. Can you imagine? You think on the movement that you want artificial arm to do, and the arm will do it!

Corrective laser eye surgery is the new innovation on eye surgery. Vision can be corrected to 20/20 in seconds. A rat in a lab recently recovered its sight by a stem cell procedure. Science, in itself, is a miracle.

The Miracle of Life

Life is the greatest thing on earth. Nothing happens without life. The miracle of life will always rank on top in the chart of miracles. Every time that a new child is born into the world, those expecting it will rejoice.

Millions of dollars are spent every year in treatments such as in-vitro-fertilization, and other modern treatments for people who want to have children, but can't.

When my wife and I were first married in 1986, we expected to have children. However, it did not happen immediately.

There was nothing wrong with us. We both had children from previous relationships; but it didn't happen immediately.

Finally, in our 6th year of marriage, we conceived, and on February 2, 1993, one of the coldest days in New York that year, at 7:47 in the morning, Jared Gabriel was born in Keller Army Hospital, West Point, New York.

Twenty years later, I continue giving thanks to God for the miracle, and enjoying the happiness of our first child together. Now, our second son did not wait! On July 20, 1994, only seventeen months after Jared was born, Caleb Emanuel came into this world with resounding noise!

I don't say it was unexpected, although we tried to plan naturally not to have another child too soon. Well, it did not work; Caleb is here, and he is here to stay! Our two boys are two of the five joys of our life.

From Death, to Life

For some, a person raised from the dead is the greatest miracle of all. Many people were raised from the dead in the Bible. In the book of Acts, Chapter 9 and verses 36-43, Peter raised a woman from the dead.

This woman lived in the city of Joppa, and was a disciple of Christ, full of good deeds and charitable works. She was also a talented seamstress who made and sold beautiful coats and garments. But she got sick, and died.

Some of the disciples in Joppa knew that Peter the apostle was nearby in a city called Lydia, and they sent for him, knowing that Christ placed a great anointing on Peter. He came, and raised her from the dead. This miracle was known throughout all Joppa, and many *believed* in the Lord; life begets life!

On another occasion, a good friend of Jesus, Lazarus by name, was sick unto death. This Lazarus was the brother of Martha and Mary. Mary was the one who anointed Jesus with fine ointment and wiped off His feet with her hair. When Jesus heard that His friend was sick, He said:

"This sickness is not unto death, but for the glory of God, that the Son of God might be glorified thereby" (John 11:4).

You see, Christ knew that Lazarus would die, but was using this as an opportunity for a miracle so that people could believe that He was the Son of God, that He was life, and that He had power over death. He waited for two more days where He was, giving time for Lazarus to die. In verse 11, He told the disciples:

"Our friend Lazarus sleeps; but I go, that I make awake him out of his sleep."

Isn't it wonderful that when we are in Christ, our death is not final, but we are simply *sleeping*, waiting for Him to wake us up from our sleep?

However, an awesome revelation on these miracles of raising people from death is that, although great miracles, to raise people from death is not the greatest miracle of all. These people were simply *revived*, but not *resurrected*. In the same way that people are revived through CPR after they are pronounced clinically dead, these people were revived, brought back to life, but not *resurrected*; all these people *died* again!

But the *resurrection*. Ah, the resurrection! What a glorious time that will be. No more death! On that day, all the dead in Christ shall rise first to meet the Lord in the air, and then all that are still living will follow up and will be with the Lord forever (1 Thess. 4:16-18). I think that people can be revived many times, but resurrected…only once!

Lazarus died before Jesus arrived at the city. In fact, he had been buried for four days now, and the Bible says that he stank. When Jesus finally came, Martha, believing that if Jesus had come before Lazarus' death He could have healed him, said to Jesus:

"Lord, if you had been here, my brother had not died. But I know that even now, whatsoever You ask God, He will give You."

Jesus said unto her, "Thy brother shall rise again."

Martha said unto Him, "I know that he shall rise again in the resurrection at the last day."

Jesus said unto her, "I am the resurrection, and the life: he that believes in Me, though he were dead, yet he shall live. And whosoever live and believes in me shall never die. Do you believe this?" (John 11:21-26 NKJ)

When Jesus told Martha that Lazarus should rise again (v. 23), He was not referring to Lazarus coming back from death on *that* day, but to the resurrection at the *last* day, when He *will* come for those who died in Him (1 Thess. 4:16-18). He is the resurrection, and the life. And whosoever believes in Him, even if he dies (in this life), shall live again forever, to die no more; that is the resurrection (vs. 25-26). These revivals were for a season, but the people *died* (ceased to physically exist) again.

Now, while Martha was the first one of the sisters to run and meet Jesus, Mary was still at home. It was Mary also who sat at Jesus' feet to hear Him when He came to visit them in the house; it was Mary the one that sat at Jesus' feet when they were near Lazarus' tomb, and it was Mary's weeping that troubled Jesus; and He wept, too.

When people pay attention to Jesus, He pays attention to them. Here we see the *Man*, Jesus, with a leadership strong as iron, but with a touch as soft as cotton, Jesus, the Son of God and God Himself, wept!

Jesus had compassion [love] for His people. The Bible says that God is full of compassion. Talking about God's compassion for His chosen people, Israel, the Bible says:

"But He [God], being full of compassion, forgave their iniquity, and did not destroy them" (Ps. 78:38).

The miracles of God come from His compassion [love] for His people. A leader who has no compassion will lead his people just for a little while, but his leadership will perish.

Every kingdom that has not been built on the foundation of compassion, fell. The Roman Empire, the Syrian Empire, Iraq, Russia, some of the kingdoms in Africa; and the list is infinite.

"But You, O Lord, are a God full of compassion, and are gracious; longsuffering and abundant in mercy and truth" (Ps. 86:15).

The unlimited grace and mercy of God, linked to the faith of the believers, are the catalysts for God's miracles. The grace of God is similar to the space in the cargo wagon of an eighteen-wheeler; it is unlimited.

As deep as the load you can put into the wagon is, equally deep is the grace of God for us. The more you sin and *truly* repent, the more He forgives you. The God of the Old Testament was as full of compassion [love] as the God of the New Testament is:

"But when He saw the multitudes, He was moved with compassion for them, because they were weary [harassed] and scattered, like sheep having no shepherd" (Matt. 9:36). That compassion is really translated in love, for God is love (1 John 4:8).

In the book of Mark, Chapter 10, we have the story of a rich young ruler seeking counsel from Christ. This young ruler was a keeper of the law, and he thought that his zeal for the law was enough for him to enter into the kingdom of God. But Jesus, knowing how wrong the young ruler was, had compassion for him, *loved* him and said to him:

"One thing you lack: Go your way, sell whatever you have and give to the poor, and you will have treasures in heaven; and come, take up the cross, and follow Me" (Mk. 10:21, NKJ). What is the cross of Christ? The love of God:

"For God so *loved* the world that He *gave* His only begotten Son, that whosoever believes in Him should not perish but have everlasting life" (John 3:16, NKJ). The love of God is the action that will lead you to love, and to *give*.

Verse 22 says that the young man was sad at this word and went away sorrowful, for he had great possessions. But the truth is that this man really didn't have possessions, because he was not in control of the possessions: the possessions *had* him! He had no love to give, because his love was in his possessions.

Jesus had love for the people, and was not afraid to show it. Love produces *life*. If you want to be a leader in like manner of God, if you want to produce *life*, have compassion [love] for others; show it! These are the two great commandments of Christ:

"You shall love the Lord your God with all your heart, with all your soul, and with your entire mind. This is the first great commandment. And the second is like it: You shall love your neighbor as yourself. On these two commandments hang all the Law and the prophets" (Matt. 22:37-40, NKJ).

Miracles reveal the presence of God, even to them that do not have a revelation of Who He is. In the Old Testament, the people, including His people, did not have a revelation of Who this God was. When they saw Him, they did not know right away it was Him, as it happened in Gen. 18:1-5.

When Abraham saw the *three* men, he greeted them as it was the custom in those days. He did not know immediately that these were two angels and the Lord Himself; a theophany, a pre-incarnated revelation of the Lord Jesus Christ.

To call visitors *Lord*, it was a sign of honor and respect conceded to guests and strangers, as when we address unknown men, not by name, but as *Sir* (Gen 18:1-3).

This is customary, both in ancient and modern Israel and the Middle East. Nothing was too good for the guest. The Bible warns us not to be forgetful to entertain strangers, because in doing so we may be entertaining angels unaware (Heb. 13:2), as Abraham did.

All the miracles that God did through Moses to Pharaoh, king of Egypt were to show Pharaoh that indeed God was the God of Israel, and that He, and not Pharaoh, was in control of the world. Not only was He the God of Israel, but He was the God of the entire world (Exodus 4:5; Deut. 34:10-12).

The purpose of the miracles in the Old Testament was to glorify the presence of God; the purpose of the miracles in the New Testament was to glorify the presence of Jesus Christ.

Peter Walks on Water

This next miracle has no parallel in history. This miracle exceeds all expectations, and defies more than one natural law. It's a miracle that I doubt will be repeated in our lifetime. It happened only once in the Bible. The Red Sea and the Jordan River were parted, and people walked on dry land; but Peter *walked* on water!

If we compare this with other miracles in the Bible, we can see that there have been more than one instance of blind people seeing again, of lame people walking, or lepers made clean, or people brought back to life. But this miracle happened only once! Peter, the man, *walked* on water. Can a man walk on water? If you think that it's easy, try it!

An Internet article tells the story of an evangelist who drowned trying to walk on water:

"An evangelist who tried replicating Jesus' miracle of walking on water, has reportedly drowned off the western coast of Africa."

"Pastor Frank Kabele, 35, told his congregation he could repeat the biblical miracle, and he attempted it from a beach in Gabon's capital of Libreville. He told church goers he had a revelation that if he had enough faith, he could walk on water like Jesus, an eyewitness told the Glasgow Daily Record.

"He took his congregation to the beach saying he would walk across the Komo estuary, which takes 20 minutes by boat to cross. He walked into the water, which soon passed over his head…and never came back! " (http://www.wnd.com/news/article.asp?ARTICLE_ID=51760)

I researched for information on the possibility of a man walking on water, and I could not find any record of anyone walking on water. The 2002 edition of the ***Guinness Book of World Records*** recorded Remy Brika, a French man that *walked* across the Atlantic Ocean; the only thing is, he wore water skies thirteen feet, nine inches long!

Many try to explain this miracle from different perspectives. Some say Jesus was walking by the sea, not on the water. How is it when Peter asked Jesus to allow him to go to Him, Peter gets out of the boat, *in the middle of the sea*, and begins to walk on the water?

Whether Jesus was walking by the seashore or in the middle of the sea, the point is Peter got out of the boat and *began* to walk on water. There is no other way to explain Peter walking on water, except a miracle.

Others say that atmospheric conditions caused the Sea of Galilee to turn to ice on the particular stretch of water Peter was walking on; how convenient. Jesus walked on water... but Peter slid on ice!

The temperature in that particular area never gets cold enough to turn water into ice. The boat got there by water, not by breaking through ice. When Peter launched onto the water, he began sinking into water, not *sliding* on ice. There was a storm, with strong winds and rain. How difficult is it for some of us to accept the miraculous in Jesus!

"Now in the fourth watch of the night Jesus went to them, walking on the sea. And when the disciples saw Him walking on the sea, they were troubled, saying, 'It is a ghost!' And they cried out for fear. But immediately Jesus spoke to them, saying, 'Be of good cheer! It is I; do not be afraid.'

"And Peter answered Him and said, "Lord, if it's You, command me to come to You on the water." So Jesus said, "Come."

"And when Peter had come down out of the boat, *he* walked on the water to go to Jesus. But when he saw that the wind was boisterous, he was afraid; and *beginning* to sink, he cried out, saying, "Lord, save me!" And immediately Jesus stretched out His hand and caught him, and said to him, "O you of little faith, why did you doubt?" And when they got into the boat, the wind ceased" (Matt. 14:25-32).

It really takes God's revelation and faith to understand an experience like this. When Peter asked Jesus to let him come to Him on the water, Jesus answered, "Come." This *come* is the same come that Jesus used in John 7:37(b) when He says:

"If any man is thirsty, let him come to me and drink..."

And it's the same *come* that Jesus used when He said:

"Come to Me, you who labor and are heavy laden, and I'll give you rest" (Matt. 11:28).

This word *come* was an inclusive word, applicable to anyone who wished to respond. If the rest of the disciples in the boat had responded and launched into the water, all would have walked on water, but only one had the audacity to launch out.

Peter jumped into the water on a word: *come*. And he began walking on water. He did not really *begin* to sink; he began to walk on water! But here is the greatness of this miracle. When you start reading about it, immediately your eyes catch Jesus walking on the water; but that's not it. There is nothing impossible for Jesus.

If He was able to lay down His own life and pick it up again after three days, what was it for Him to walk on water? No, the greatness of this miracle is that *Peter* walked on water!

The Bible says that Peter walked on the water to come to Jesus. It doesn't say that he sank, but that he *walked*. Peter was walking on the word of Jesus. Peter was walking on a word of faith. As long as he was walking on that word, he was walking on water; he was on a smooth path.

But suddenly, Peter began to pay attention to the rowdy wind, and he was afraid; he took his eyes off of Jesus, and he *began* to sink; how many of us begin walking right with Jesus, enjoying His blessings even in the midst of turmoil, to suddenly succumb to circumstances in life, and *begin* to sink?

The funny thing about this word, *begin* to sink, is that with man, no one begins to sink. The *Titanic* began to sink; there was a process. But with man, if you don't know how to swim, you'll sink, at once.

There is no such thing as beginning to sink. If you know how to swim, you'll stay afloat until you get tired and then, if not rescued, you'll sink. You'll not *begin* to sink, but you'll sink!

When I see this word *begin*, I see a metaphor, I see a divine process. This *beginning* to sink, to me, is God giving us time to repent, to get our act together, to change our minds, even in the midst of sin. It's God saying:

"Hey, I'm giving you a chance; get hold of the *plank* (faith) floating around you, and float for a little while, until I send in rescue. Better yet, I'll come down myself and rescue you."

When you get hold to the *plank*, Jesus will stretch out His hands and will *rescue* you; He will save you. That's the love that He has for you!

I personally believe that walking on water is the greatest physical miracle the human eye has ever *seen*. This miracle is so supernatural that it was never repeated in the Bible, and I believe it will never be, as other miracles have. It is second only to the second coming of our Lord Jesus Christ, when He will break the heavens with a shout of trumpets to receive us into glory.

On that day, people will walk on water again, because the Bible says that the dead in Christ shall rise first. All the Christians who died in the seas and are still there will rise from the waters to meet the Lord in the air. They will not only walk on water, but will leap out of it! That will be the greatest event to see ever (1 Thess. 4:16-18).

Which is the greatest miracle of all? We can study all the miracles in the Bible, and I don't believe we will ever agree on any particular miracle. Everyone will see each miracle based on their own experience, need, and knowledge of God.

However, I think no one will disagree that the following is the greatest miracle of all. It has no comparison with anything else:

THE GREATEST MIRACLE OF ALL

"Though I speak with the tongues of men and of angels, but have not love, I have become sounding brass or a clanging cymbal. And though I have the gift of prophecy, and understand all mysteries and all knowledge, and though I have all faith, so that I could remove mountains, but have not love, I am And though I bestow all my goods to feed the poor, and though I give my body to be burned, but have not love, it profits me nothing.

Love suffers long and is kind; love does not envy; love does not parade itself, is not puffed up; does not behave rudely, does not seek its own, is not provoked, thinks no evil; does not rejoice in iniquity, but rejoices in the truth; bears all things, believes all things, hopes all things, endures all things.

Love never fails. But whether there are prophecies, they will fail; whether there are tongues, they will cease; whether there is knowledge, it will vanish away. For we know in part and we prophecy in part. But when that which is perfect has come, then that which is in part will be done away.

When I was a child, I spoke as a child, I understood as a child, I thought as a child; but when I became a man, I put away

childish things. For now we see in a mirror, dimly, but then face to face. Now I know in part, but then I shall know just as I also am known.
And now abide faith, hope, and love, these three; but the greatest of these is LOVE"(1 Corinthians 13, NKJ).

Saturday, 9 December 2006 was the presentation of the most prestigious award in college football, the Heisman Trophy, presented to Troy Smith, Ohio State University quarterback, as the Most Valuable college football player in 2006. Jim Tressel, Troy's football coach, was interviewed and the question was asked of him:

"What did you learned by coaching Troy?"

"I did not learn anything, but I did re-learn that love is the greatest force that there is."

Troy Smith overcame a troubled childhood through the *love* of men and women God placed in his life, especially his high school coach, who Troy recognizes as the greatest influence in his life.

It was the miracle of love that turned Troy's life around, to the extent of becoming the Heisman Trophy winner, the most prestigious award in college football. Only the love of God can turn around troubled lives like Troy's, and mine; and He can turn yours, too, if you give Him a chance!

He can perform a miracle in your life. Miracles happen when we intercede for others, as Troy's coaches interceded for him.

LOVE, THE GREATEST MIRACLE OF ALL

Nothing can exceed the greatness of love. When I look at the spiritual gifts that God has placed in the lives of people, I see them as the greatest manifestations of God's power in them. And yet, none of these gifts can change the lives of men as love can.

It was love, the love of God for humanity that changed the entire world with the death and resurrection of Jesus Christ (John 3:16). The spiritual gifts are only a manifestation of God's power, but love is His nature, it's Himself:

"He that doesn't love does not know God, because God is love" (1 John 4:8).

It is reciprocal in us to love one another, simply because God loves us. The only way to show that God is in us is by loving one another. No one has seen God, and yet we say that we love Him. But if we can't love our *neighbor,* whom we see, the love of God is not in us. Only by loving one another can we show that the love of God dwells in us. 1 John 4:11-12 says:

"Beloved, if God so loved us, we ought also to love one another. No one has seen God at any time. If we love one another, God abides in us, and His love has been perfected in us.

"And, if someone says, 'I love God' and hates his brother, he is a liar: for he who does not love his brother whom he has seen, how can he love God whom he has not seen?" (1 John 4:20)

God places no greater emphasis on anything else than the emphasis He places on love: "You shall love the Lord your God with all your heart, and with all your soul, and with your entire mind." He calls it the great commandment (Matt. 22:37-38).

And His second greatest commandment is similar, "You shall love your neighbor as yourself" (v.39). Everything God does emanates from love, because He is love.

God so loved us so much, that He sent His only Son to die for us, that we might live through Him. No one loves us as God does. And He is asking us to love our neighbor, friend or enemy, as He loves us. That's the greatness (and simplicity) of God's love!

Love shines in the midst of pain and suffering. Fear is the antithesis of strength. Fear is the most destructive force on earth, because fear is accompanied by anguish, pain and suffering. But love is the greatest life-producing force. Love throws out fear.

There is no fear in love (1 John 4:18). God did not give us the spirit of fear, but of power, and of *love*, and of a sound mind (2 Tim. 1:7). The love of God is the kind of mature, perfect love that casts out all fear. And because there is no fear in love, and no faith in fear, there is therefore strength in love: the strength of God.

Through strength we conquer; through fear we are defeated. There is nothing we cannot conquer through love. God is love. Love is the universal miracle that keeps everything together. It is the force that binds the souls of people one to another. It is the axis by which the universe turns; love is the only thing in the world that everyone wants; everyone wants to be loved! *'What's love got to do with it?'* **Everything!**

Pastor Clinton Utterbach, pastor of Redeeming Love Christian Center in Nanuet, New York, wrote a song that says, "Love is not a feeling but an action." And indeed, it is! A double-edged sword action: *giving*, and *receiving*. No one can explain love. All one can do is to *give* it, and someone else has to *receive* it.

When you give love, you know it because virtue, grace, and compassion flow *out* of you. And when you receive love, you know it because virtue, grace, and compassion flow *into* you. That's the only way to explain it! It's different; it is something that when you experience it for the first time, you will never be the same again. Everybody wants and needs love.

Many teens and young boys and girls join gangs because they feel *loved* by other gang members. But it is difficult for them to know what real love is, the love of God, because they look for love in the wrong place and for the wrong kind of love; the other gang members are in the same boat!

They themselves cannot give love, because they don't know love; they haven't been shown the love of God. Why do you think they joined the gangs in the first place? But when you find the love of God, as Nicky Cruz found it, your life will be changed forever!

When we hear about child molesters and serial killers, we think of them as the scum of the earth, as the lowest on earth. It's very difficult for us to see them with eyes of compassion; it's very difficult for us to love them.

And, yet, this scum is the scum that Christ died for. Some of us were scum before we met Jesus. Yet, He loved us, and died for us!

These are the people who God sacrificed His only Son for. It's easy to love the lovable, and to forgive the forgivable. But when it comes to loving the unlovable and forgiving the unforgivable, it takes the love of God to do it. We once were unlovable and unforgivable; but He loved us, and forgave us…in spite of ourselves!

We don't understand that these people are victims of a society that didn't love them. If you hear their stories, you'll probably find a childhood filled with unloving parents; you'll find abused children. All they are seeking for is love, the love of God through us. Love can change them, as it changed us.

You cannot give what you don't have. If they had no love, they cannot give love. But, are we better than they are?

"For all have sinned, and have come short of the glory of God" (Ro. 3:23). If we were better, we would have been able to forgive them, as Jesus forgave us.

"If we confess our sins, He is faithful and just to forgive our sins, and to cleanse us from all unrighteousness" (1 John 1:9).

When Jesus died on the cross, there were two thieves, *scum*, crucified with Him. One of the thieves mocked the Son of God, but the other repented. Jesus, having compassion [love] not only forgave him, but promised that he would be in paradise with Him on that same day.

It didn't take a special condition for Jesus to forgive him: only the thief's repentance! (Lu. 23:39-43) And those who crucified Him, He also forgave them; no conditions; "Father, forgive them; for they know not what they do" (Lu. 23:34).

Why can't we do that? I will tell you why: because we do not always operate in the love of God. We sometimes walk in our own self-righteousness. We have to add our own plans and doctrine to the doctrine and plan of salvation of God.

He places no conditions, but we do. Where He says go and sin no more, we say do this, or do that, and then you will be forgiven. Are we greater that God? Are we better than the one asking us for forgiveness?

When we explore the 13th Chapter of 1 Corinthians, we are able to *see* and *feel* the magnificence and excellence of God's love.

"If we are able to speak in other [spiritual] tongues, if we are able to explain or interpret all the mysteries of the world, if we are able to move mountains with our faith but have no love, it profits nothing for us."

If am the richest person in the world, richer than Bill Gates, and am able to give all that money to the poor, but have not love, I have really given in vain; it profits me nothing before God. It will make the poor happy, but it will profit me nothing. When Jesus died in the cross, it was not simply Him giving His body for us; it was much more than that: it was love!

When Jesus was in Gethsemane, He had the chance to give up and not die. He was the Son of God, and He could have gone back to heaven with the Father. God, the Father, would have found another way to save us. But in Gethsemane, Jesus found that the love the Father had for us, and His obedience to the Father, were exceedingly greater than the suffering of the death He was about to face. He prayed to the Father not to let Him die:

"Father, if it is Your will, take this cup away from Me; nevertheless not My will, but Yours, be done" (Luke 22:42).

He did not want to face a death reserved only for the worst. It was a curse then to die hanging on a cross. His agony was so great that His sweat was as great drops of blood falling to the ground.

It was so spiritually painful that an angel had to come down from heaven and minister to Him. But even in the midst of His agony, He found strength in the love of the Father for us and in His love for the Father and for us, and He accepted the will of the Father to die for us (Luke 22:39-44). I can imagine Him saying:

"Father, I don't want to die this horrible death. What have I done to deserve it?"

But then, I can picture Him looking beyond His own death, *loving* us; seeing *your* face, and *my* face, dying in hell, lost in eternal damnation; I can *hear* Him pleading with the Father:

"Father, I can't see the people that You love dying and going to hell. I love you so much, and I know You love them so much, and I love them so that I want not My will, but Yours to be done. I want Our love to be eternal. I'll die for them!"

Could there be a greater love? The Bible says that no greater love has anyone than to give his life for a friend. Jesus is your friend, your best friend, the only one who gave His life for you. My former First Lady, Pastor Tina Tate says:

"Jesus is the only one that has never hurt anyone." So true! This supreme, selfless act of sacrifice of Jesus was not only giving, but it was God's nature, the main appearance of Him living in us. It was God making us an inward part of who He is: Love!

This love of God, the Agape kind of love, is the kind of love that places others before self. Paul explicitly speaks about it when he asks us to look not every man on his own things, but also on the things of others. In other words, be mindful of the interests of others first (Phil. 2:4).

In his *Marriage Counseling Guide*, Bishop Nate Holcomb says of Agape love:

"The Agape love has absolutely nothing to do with the object being lovable. It loves someone whether she/he is good or bad. It's centered in the will. Agape has nothing to do with the object, but with the lover."

Agape love is independent of the object. The object may not be lovable or may not love you, but you still love that person. All of us have the capacity to love this way.

Agape is the love that inspires you to love your enemy. Jesus said to do something for that person who despitefully uses and persecutes you. It's the kind of love that will cause you to love a person regardless of what the person has done to you (John 3:16; Ro. 12:9-21).

This is the kind of love that transcends all barriers: color, race, gender, looks, and physical limitations. Nothing can stop this kind of love from manifesting God in the lives of people who want Him, and make you to love your enemy. God will not receive an offering from you if you are in enmity with your brother:

"Therefore, if you bring your gift to the altar, and there you remember that your brother has something against you, leave your gift there before the altar, and go your way. First be reconciled with your brother, and then come and offer our gift" (Matt. 5:23-24).

This kind of love, Agape love, is the love that can compel a mother to forgive her son's killer:

Michelle Richardson-Patterson is the mother of ten children, eight of them living. She lived in Condon Terrace in Southeast Washington, a neighborhood in constant war with its nearby neighborhood, Barry Farm Dwellings.

*In 2004, her teenage son James was murdered by nineteen-year-old Thomas Boykin, also known as "T.J." T.J. was a teen from Barry Farm Dwellings.

On June, when T.J. was sentenced, Michelle asked the judge to show mercy for him. As the people left the courtroom, Michelle and Pearl, Boykin's mother, embraced and prayed. They had become friends and they visited Boykin at jail together.

"When I looked at that young man, I saw someone who could have a second chance to rehabilitate himself and come out and be a powerful – and I mean a powerful – member of society; but most of all, a powerful servant of God. That's what I saw," Richardson-Patterson said about the jail visit.

"I didn't really see somebody, 'Oh, you killed my son; you ought to be dead.' And I am just a firm believer, if God can forgive me all the stuff I've done, then why can't I forgive somebody else?"

In a society in which relatives of murdered victims think only in ways to avenge their dead, in a time in which they go to the death chamber just to see the killers suffer while they are executed and wish them eternal hell, Michelle chose a better way: forgiveness! God is love, and there is forgiveness in love. *(www.washingtonpost.com, 2004.)

In 2007, Thomas Bart Whitaker was convicted of murder in the first degree for plotting the death of his mother, father and younger brother.

On December 2003, after celebrating Bart's "graduation" from college, and as they returned home, they found themselves in the midst of a shootout that left his mother and younger brother dead, and his father, Kent wounded. A "burglar" was waiting for them at home, and opened fire as they enter their home.

Bart's himself was "wounded" in a struggle with the killer. He and Kent were the only survivors. After two years of investigation, it was found that Bart has not graduated from college, had been lying to his parents, and had plotted more than once to kill his parents. He succeeded in killing his mother and brother, but his father survived the attempt.

In his book, "Murder by Family: The True Story of a Son's Treachery and a Father's Forgiveness," Kent Whitaker speaks about how, after praying to God and asking for guidance, God told him to forgive his son, and he forgave him. Only through the love of God can a father forgive the killer of his wife and son, even if the killer is his other son; only the love of God!

It is said that Max Lucado had one of the greatest experiences of his life while visiting poor countries. He visited the poor streets where young girls were sold as prostitutes by street pimps.

He saw some of these little girls and invited them to come to his room at night. When night came and the girls came to his hotel room ready to *work*, they found the greatest surprise of their young lives.

Prior to their arrival, Max ordered ice cream and rented nice clean movies. When the girls came to the room, he asked them to sit on the bed; he put the movies on, and treated them with delicious ice cream. For the entire night, the girls watched movies, ate ice cream, watched movies, laughed, and fell asleep.

For one night, those girls were what God created them to be: His little girls, having fun and enjoying His creation. True, the next morning they would go back to become what sinful men had made them to be. But for that night they were the little children of God, something that no one could ever take away from them. And all because of the love of God that one man had for them!

Even Christ, who was God in the flesh, took upon Him the form of man and became less than God. He stripped off His majesty and humbled Himself even unto death, the death on the cross, for us (Phil.2:4-8).

And all was done in the name of love:

"For God so loved the world that He gave His only begotten Son, that *whosoever* believes in Him should not perish, but have everlasting life." (John 3:16.) We are that whosoever!

Love is longsuffering. Love has the patience to wait, even when you don't want to wait. Love has the ability to love the unlovable, to forgive the unforgivable, and to restore lost relationships.

UNCONDITIONAL FORGIVENESS

The Restoration of Job

Job was the son of Nahor. He was a real person, also named in the book of Ezekiel, 14:14 and in James, 5:11. Job was a righteous man.

"There was a man in the land of Uz, whose name was Job: and that man was blameless and upright, and one who feared God and shunned evil" (Job 1:1).

At the time, there was not a man as faithful as Job. He had a family of seven sons and three daughters, and was very rich. The Lord had blessed him mightily because of his faithfulness to God. But Satan did not like Job, and was after him, to destroy him. One day, as God had a conversation with Satan, and knowing his intentions, God offered Job to Satan to be tested:

"Have you considered my servant Job, that there is none like him on the earth, a blameless and upright man, one that fears God and shuns evil?" (Job 1:8; 2:3). God is calling Job a righteous man, one who shuns evil (sin).

If you read the book of Job, you will see all the calamities and suffering he went through at the hands of Satan, only because he loved God, and God loved him. Satan killed all Job's children, and destroyed his possessions. But in all this, Job never sinned or cursed God. In the end, God blessed and restored Job abundantly, with much more than he had before:

"So the Lord blessed the latter end of Job more than his beginning: for he had fourteen thousand sheep, and six thousand camels, and a thousand yoke of oxen, and a thousand she-asses. He also had seven more sons and three daughters" (Job, 42:12-13). This was the miraculous of God at work; His love! And He can do it for us, too!

The Pardon of Onesimus

Philemon was a Christian from the city of Colosse, and a good friend of Paul, the apostle of Jesus Christ. He had a slave, Onesimus, who had robbed him and fled to Rome. In Rome, Onesimus met Paul and was converted to Christianity.

Paul wrote a letter to his friend Philemon, asking him to forgive Onesimus. In asking, Paul made mention of the love Philemon had for the Lord Jesus and for all the saints, love that would lead him to forgive his former slave, who in time past was unprofitable to Philemon, but now profitable not only to his master, but to Paul and to the Gospel.

Paul knew it was only through the love of Jesus Christ that Philemon could forgive Onesimus. It is not easy to forgive someone you have trusted and who betrayed you. But when the love of God is in you, there is nothing good you cannot do, even to forgive your enemy, if you purpose in your heart to do it. Not only did Paul ask Philemon to forgive Onesimus, but he asked him to restore him. Not as a servant, but as a beloved brother in the faith. Paul tells Philemon:

"If he has wronged you, or if he owes anything to you, put it on my account; don't forget that you owe me your own self" (Phi., Vs 16-19).

In his farewell to Philemon, vs. 24, Paul also sent greetings from Marcus. Who was Marcus? Marcus was John Mark, the same one who in Acts 15:36-41 caused a breach between Barnabas and Paul.

Paul was going on a missionary journey with Barnabas, who wanted to take John Mark with them. But Paul did not want to take him because Mark had abandoned them in Pamphylia, and did not go with them to the work of the Lord:

"And the contention was so sharp between them, that they departed asunder one from the other: and so Barnabas took Mark, and sailed into Cyprus" (Acts 15:36-41).

Did Paul and John Mark remain angry with one another forever? No! The love of God is greater than that. The love of God will never allow you to remain angry with your brethren, if His love is in you. In the second letter that Paul wrote to the young pastor Timothy, Paul says:

"Only Luke is with me. Get *Mark* and bring him with you, for he is useful to me for ministry" (2 Tim 4:11). Paul had the heart to forgive his *brother* John Mark and restore him to full fellowship with him, and to the work of the Gospel. Marcus' mistake was remembered by Paul no more. At the first opportunity, the love of God was triumphant and manifested through Paul. We all sin and fall short of the glory of God. If God forgives and restores us, are we not to forgive and restore our brethren?

Wasn't that what Jesus did? Didn't He take our sins on the cross and pay with His own life, so we would not have to die for our own sins? He who knew no sin became sin for us, and restored us to full fellowship with the Father, only because of His love.

Sometimes restoration takes place immediately, as with the lost son in the parable in Luke Chapter 15. Other times, there is a process of proving oneself once more, as in the case of Onesimus and John Mark. Paul says of Onesimus:

"I appeal to you for my son Onesimus, whom I have begotten while in my chains, which once *was* unprofitable to you, but now *is* profitable to you and to me" (Phi., Vs. 10-11).

Of John Mark he says:

"Only Luke is with me. Get Mark and bring him with you, for he is useful to me for ministry" (2 Tim. 4:11).

By this, it is evident that both Onesimus and John Mark have done something to prove their profitability again. Before, Paul refused to take Mark with him; Mark abandoned him (Acts 15:36-41). But now, Paul wanted Mark again with him. And Onesimus was sent back to work with his owner, now a *changed* man. In both cases, there was a time of proving. But when the *season* had come, they were received and restored. God will not abandon you, but will bid you to come, and He will receive you. How many times? Seventy times seven!

In other words, as many times as it's needed, as long as there is genuine repentance. Remember, we all have sinned and have fallen short of the glory of God, but He is always willing to forgive us (1 John 1:9). Then can we, who were loved unconditionally, forgiven much and restored, forgive and restore our brethren for the sake of the love of Jesus? I think we can! The love of Jesus can transcend any barrier.

Jesus never hated Judas Iscariot, who betrayed Him. He loved him, and made him part of His fellowship, of the chosen twelve, though He knew who Judas was: a thief, a traitor who would betray and sell Him. If Jesus loved Judas, can we not love our brethren, even our enemies?

I'm truly convinced that there is no true forgiveness without restoration. Though Job did not really sin when Satan tempted him and destroyed all he had, including his family, God restored him seven-fold what he previously had before his calamities: family, money, property, and a good life even in his old age (Job, 42:12-17).

When Paul forgave John Mark, not only did he forgive him, but he restored him to his work as an evangelist with him. When Paul asked Philemon to forgive his own slave, Onesimus, not only did he ask to forgive him, but to receive him back. No longer as a slave, but rather as a brother in the work of the Lord Jesus Christ.

There was not only restoration, but exaltation to a higher office. Before, Onesimus was a slave and a thief; now, Paul is asking Philemon to receive him as a fellow worker in the Gospel. That is the love of God!

The Lost Son

Luke Chapter 15 gives what I consider one of the greatest parables in the Bible, one of the greatest examples of God's love, forgiveness and restoration. The story of the lost son is a more intimate, compelling one; it is the story of a father and his two sons. One day, the youngest son decided to ask the father for his inheritance. This story is very peculiar.

First, the son asked for his inheritance while still living at his father's home, which was kind of unusual. Routinely, it's the father who decides when to pass on the inheritance, as the children become of age or move out of home in good terms.

Secondly, his father was still alive. Typically, inheritances are to be received when the parents die, or become very old and can't manage the responsibility of property or money. In some cases, trustees are put in place until children reach age of accountability.

This father decided to give him his portion, and the young man went on a spending journey. Not only did he spend his portion, the hard earned money of his father, but he wasted it on riotous, prodigal living. In other words, he spent the money in parties, alcohol and women (Lu. 15:13).

It is worth noticing that the father divided *to them* his livelihood; he gave both sons their inheritance, but only one went out to squander it. Even in this act we see the love of this father, who, because of the doggedness of one son, decided to give both sons their inheritance. This father did not withhold anything good from his children. Isn't this God-like?

"For the Lord God is a sun and shield, the Lord will give grace and glory, no good thing will He withhold from those who walk uprightly" (Ps. 84:11).

The Bible says that the younger son gathered his possessions and traveled to a far country and wasted all his possessions. To make it worse, as soon as he spent all his money, there was a famine in the land where he was living. He began working for a farmer of that country, tending the swine; he was hungry, but no one gave him anything to eat.

To make the story short, when he saw that even the swine ate better than him, he came [to his senses] and decided to go back to his father and ask him for forgiveness. But when the father saw him from afar, he had compassion [love] and ran and fell on his neck and kissed him.

He asked his father for forgiveness, but before he could finish his confession, the father ordered his servants to bring the best robe, and put it in on him, and a ring on his finger, and sandals on his feet. And he killed the *fattest* calf and threw a party for him in celebration.

"For this my son was dead and is alive again: he was lost and is found: and they began to be merry" (Lu. 15:11-24).

It is evident that the father never lost hope in this son; he was waiting for him to come back, and *saw* him from *afar*. He had loved him, he had raised him well, and he knew that one day he would repent and return home. That's the love of a good father; it never gives up hope!

When the son asked for forgiveness, the father didn't speak, but simply forgave him, loved him, and restored him to his old relationship as a son.

In one of his messages, a former pastor was making an analogy about one's anointing, or grace to do ministry:

"When we lose the anointing, three things we must do in order to restore back the lost anointing: remember where we lost it, repent that we lost it, and go back to the one who gave you the anointing: God."

In the parable of the lost son, the same analogy can be applied to sin: the son remembered where he sinned, he repented of his sin, and he went back to the one who gave him his blessings, his *father*.

What did he received in return? The same or even greater love than the love he had before he left *home*. Home really represents a life in Christ, while the *world* represents a sinful life.

That's God. That is what God does for us. He never loses hope in us. When we sin, when we backslide He calls us back, and waits for us to repent and return to Him, and He forgives us, and He loves us, and He restores us to a greater fellowship with Him (Jer. 3:22; Hos. 14:4).

Is there any greater love than this? And yet, this is the love God has put in us. This is the example Jesus left for us, that we may walk in His steps. If we can't love the way Jesus loved, we are not of Him; we are not of God,

"Beloved, let us love one another, for love is of God; and everyone who loves is born of God and knows God. He who does not love does not know God, for God is love" (1 John 4:7-8).

The Woman Caught in Adultery

The Gospel of John gives us one of the most awe-inspiring examples of the compassion, the righteousness, and the love of Jesus.

One day, as Jesus came down from the Mount of Olives early in the morning, and after a day of great debate between the Pharisees, who didn't believe that He was the Christ and the people who believed He was the Christ, He came into the temple and the people came with Him, to hear His wisdom.

But the Scribes and the Pharisees, the lawyers and religious rulers of the Jews, brought to Him a woman who was caught in the act of adultery. When they had placed her in the midst of the congregation, they asked Him if they could stone her to death, because the Law of Moses commanded to do so. They did this to test Him, to see if they could find something to accuse Him of breaking the Law.

But Jesus, knowing their intentions, stooped down and began to write on the ground, as if He did not hear them. When they insisted, He lifted His eyes and told them:

"He who is without sin among you, let him throw a stone at her first." And He stooped down and continued writing on the ground.

When the accusers heard it, convicted in their minds of their own sins, they dropped the rocks on the ground and began to leave one by one, until there was no one else but Jesus and the woman. Then He said to her, "Woman, where are those accusers of yours? Has no one condemned you?"

She said, "No one, Lord."

And Jesus said to her, "Neither do I condemn you; go and sin no more."

Just like that, Jesus forgave her and sent her on her way. (John 8:1-11) No condemnation, no penitence; just forgiveness. That is the mind and the heart of God and that is the mind that Paul asks us to have.

"Let this mind be in you which was also in Christ Jesus." (Phil. 2:5).

If we have the mind of Christ, we will think like Him and we will love like Him. We'll not condemn or judge anyone, lest we be judged and condemned ourselves. We all have sinned and come short of the glory of God, so what gives us the right to judge others, and to walk in un-forgiveness?

Jesus Christ, the righteous one, the sinless one forgave without conditions, loved unconditionally. Let us do the same with our neighbor, that we fulfill His love in us. Everyone who loves is born of God and knows God.

Love is the nature of God. This is the greatest miracle of all, and God performs it in our lives every day; He loves us daily. Every new day the love of God is renewed in us. It happens over and over again!

If you want to be partaker of the greatest miracle of all, **love one another**! Bishop Nate Holcomb says about love:

"There is nothing we can do to make Jesus love us, and there is nothing we can do to prevent Him from loving us!"

In an episode of the popular show *Touched by An Angel*, the angel Monica said:

"God never created anything stronger than love." And, do you know why? Simply, because God is love, and God did not create Himself; therefore, He did not create love. Love…just is, because God is!

SOME MIRACLES IN MY LIFE

Now, let me tell you about some of the miracles that God has done for me. In 1986, while stationed at the US Military Academy in West Point, New York, and while a member of St. Mark's Baptist Church, a small family church in Highland Falls, NY, I met the woman who has been my wife for the past twenty-seven years, Sheila.

When I met her, I was going through the painful process of divorce. I asked her out, and she said no. Oh, that hurt! *Rejection* was not in my *vernacular*, so I got a little angry and told myself that I would never ask her out again.

Back then, a novice Christian, I didn't understand that it's not God's will for people *legally* married to date other people; but Sheila knew it! Well, my divorce went through, but I still did not ask her out again!

There was a young deacon in my church, Deacon Dwayne Williams, who was married to Sheila's cousin, Kimberly. One day I told Deacon Williams that the Lord told me that Sheila was going to call me on the weekend. He laughed. That same weekend, she called me! She told me that the Lord told her to call me.

I told her I knew she was going to call, and that she could ask Deacon Williams for confirmation. Some months later we were married, and have been married for the last 27 years, for the glory of God. That's what love does for you!

A Master's Degree

1999-2000 was a time for another miracle in my life. I retired from the Army in November 1999 after twenty-two years of service. Long before that, I tried unsuccessfully to engage in graduate education, but somehow, it did not happen.

There seemed to be obstacles always in my way for me to complete my master's degree. Finally, in November 1999, and after much prayer from my wife and me, we decided that I would apply for an eighteen-month master's in an education program offered by National-Louis University. I applied, and miraculously was accepted in the program. Some may ask:

"Where is the miraculous in someone been accepted into college? That's the norm." Well, nothing is miraculous about it, except that I applied nine months after the program had started! Not only that, but I finished the degree together with the other students.

There was a lot of catching up to do: long nights of reading, dissertations, book reports to turn in, library visits, reading books...and a thesis! But by the grace of God, I graduated in August of 2000 with a master's degree in education, with a 4.0 GPA! Wasn't that a miracle? Indeed it was!

Another miracle in my life is, well, you have it in your hands: this simple, but full of God's love book. Enjoy it, and

I pray that the Lord will perform the greatest miracle of all in your life today; even His *love*! As my former First Lady said, "If you have Him [His love], you have everything!"

POSTSCRIPT

A Beautiful Mind

In the movie "*A Beautiful Mind*," the biography of John Nash, the great American mathematician, John said:

"I have made the most important discovery of my life. It's only in the mysterious equation of *love* that logical reason can be found." Even logic is found in love!

And listen to this dialogue between *John* and *Alicia* (A Beautiful Mind):

Alicia: How big is the universe?

John: Infinite

Alicia: How do you know?

John: I know because all the data indicates it's infinite.

Alicia: But it hasn't been proven yet.

John: No.

Alicia: How do you know for sure?

John: I don't; I just believe it.

Alicia: It's the same thing with love, I guess.

You see, friends, love doesn't have to be proven, just *believed* on; love…just is!

Postscript

If at any time the enemy deceives you into believing that you have lost all faith and hope in love, go back to the first place where you found God, and He will be right there waiting for you with your newfound love.

General Colin Powell, the former Chairman of the Joint Chiefs of Staff Council, and Secretary of State, once said, "When you shake hands with a stranger, that person is not a stranger anymore."

Don't be a stranger today. Be a miracle; love someone today. Maybe the miracle you need in your life today is someone for you to love, or someone to love you.

"And now abide faith, hope and love, these three; but the greatest of these is **love**" (1 Corinthians 13:13, NKJ).

www.ingramcontent.com/pod-product-compliance
Lightning Source LLC
LaVergne TN
LVHW020448070526
838199LV00063B/4879